...Becaus

Why is there suffering'

by A.J. Ferneley

Contents:

Prologue

What, '… Because of love' does not mean.

I would prefer not to have anyone hurl this book across the room in disgust before they have even started reading it, because of its title… so a short Prologue might be necessary for some.

The danger in calling a book about suffering, "… Because of Love" is that it could instantly be taken as saying God deliberately sends suffering because God loves us and wants to teach us to be good. If I thought that was what might be meant, *I* might throw this book across the room! Suffering has sometimes been seen as a tool in God's kitbag to make us better, and he wants the *very* best for us so he uses it. Though this has been argued in many and varied ways, it is emphatically *not* what I mean! A God that deliberately sent the horrors of war and genocide and the terrible accidents that tear lives apart, as some sort of lesson, would be a monster. Much more of that to come…

What I *do* mean is, that to give a *Christian* response, not just to suffering, but to any question at all, you must start with love. If it is true that 'God is Love' (*1 John 4:8*), then love is the reason for everything, and so love is ultimately the reason why there is suffering. That, as I see it, is a Christian response. Starting anywhere else – for example, by trying to resolve a logical dilemma about an all-powerful and good God and the existence of suffering – may give some insights, but it is not a specifically *Christian* response, and that is what I want to explore.

Wrestling with this is about loving God with all your mind (*Mark 12:30*). Don't be afraid of discovering something that seems to threaten your faith. Eduard Schweizer wrote, when he was wrestling with theology,

"I was taught not to fear the truth, and never to be anxious about detecting something that seemed to endanger my faith since God was always on the side of truth and not illusion."[1] Too often Christians are afraid to wrestle with the issue of suffering. The territory seems too hostile, populated by very vocal and articulate atheists. But Christianity has always been a faith that was *born* out of reflection on suffering – the suffering of Jesus himself and how that brought hope into a world of suffering. It isn't as if we somehow hadn't thought of this idea the atheists throw at us.

Acknowledgements

This is not meant to be an academic book. You won't find extensive footnotes about where the different ideas can be explored in more depth. Though a lot of ink has been spilled for centuries on the subject, I make no attempt to give you a survey of all that has been said. Though I have a few letters after my name in the area, I can't say I really have an academic's brain. Many of the thoughts herein will be those of others that I have heard or read once upon a time, but I can't remember where I first heard them. I don't mean to plagiarise anyone though and where I can remember I will credit the ideas. But so much thought has gone into this area I doubt I could say anything completely original apart from those parts springing from personal experience.

One person in particular I will mention though, and that is my undergraduate tutor at the Roehampton Institute in the early 1990's, Michael Nevin. The basic premise that if God is love, the existence of suffering must be because of love, I learned from him.

Introduction

As a Christian minister in 21st Century England I find the most common question the dog-collar attracts is, 'Why does God allow suffering?' - or if not that exactly, some variant on the theme. Some assume God actively sends the bad things that happen and is out to get them in some way, but more often it's simply an anguished puzzlement that is held alongside faith by most of those that have it. The atheist tends to think religious believers somehow haven't thought of this, but most of them feel it very keenly. Some give up faith because they cannot find a satisfying answer – whether anything unpleasant has happened to them personally or not. Some refuse faith, they say, for the same reason. Most carry on believing, but with their questions unanswered – not really knowing where to start. This book is an attempt to give those ordinary believers (or non-believers or half-believers) a tool to help them wrestle with the questions. For the most part we will all have to carry on, myself included, with the questions ultimately unanswered, but that doesn't mean that Christian faith has nothing to say.

The day before I began writing this book I visited a couple whose 14 year old son – their only child - had died suddenly and unexpectedly from complications from a cold affecting an undiagnosed heart defect. That sort of thing happens all the time in other parts of the world, though it is shocking to us. The day after, I heard a heart rending story from the other side of the town where I ministered. An 8 month old baby had drowned in a bath when her mum popped out to get a towel or something and her bath seat had toppled over. What do you *do* with that?! Where was God?! Couldn't an almighty God have stopped the seat toppling? If he could, why didn't he? If he couldn't, what sort of God are we talking about?

As the busyness of ministry squashed out any time to write, my thoughts were put on hold, but again and again I heard in the news, stories we all hear. This question is universal. Then a member of one of my own churches – a woman in her early 40's – had a cancer, that had previously been fought off, return. A long fight led to collapsed vertebrae and a failed operation to try to improve her situation, leaving her in terrible pain. She didn't feel able to come to church any more, and didn't really want to talk to me about it, but second hand I heard her questions to others who were caring for her on the church's behalf and from their own love for her. 'Why is God doing this to me?' 'What have I done?' A friend who was supporting her asked me in anguish, 'What can I say to her?!' Anything we say has to be say-able to these people. This is much more than an intellectual puzzle.

Quite apart from our own experiences and the experiences of those we care about, people of faith are frequently, vocally and sometimes viciously attacked from without and accused of being stupid for believing in a loving God in a world such as this. As a typical example, in January 2015 in an interview, Stephen Fry was asked what he would say if he came face-to-face with God? His response was as forceful as it was clear. "How dare you?!" he said to a stunned interviewer. Then he launched into a powerful speech about how, if there were a God, he would be "utterly, utterly evil". "I'll say: 'Bone cancer in children?! What's that about?! How dare you, how dare you create a world where there is such misery that's not our fault?' It's utterly, utterly evil. Why should I respect a capricious, mean-minded, stupid god who creates a world which is so full of injustice and pain? The god who created this universe, if he created this universe, is quite clearly a maniac, an utter maniac, totally selfish. And we have to spend our lives on our knees *thanking* him! What kind of god would do that? Yes, the world is very splendid, but it also has in it insects whose whole life cycle is to burrow into the eyes of children and make them blind."[1]

There are plenty of others who say this sort of stuff, though Fry is perhaps the most articulate and well known among them for ordinary Christians who enjoy the television shows he has presented. On QI (Quite Interesting) Fry told millions of viewers about the jewel wasp. Its life cycle involves stinging a cockroach in the brain, turning it into a sort of zombie, then dragging it by the antenna into a hole, packing it in, and laying eggs next to it. The larvae then eat the cockroach from the inside out in a very specific order, keeping it alive as long as possible, as cockroach meat goes off very quickly in the warmth. As Fry said, how the hell could a benign creator who loves all he has made come up with *that*?! If there is a God how do we end up living in a world where there are such things as bone cancer and jewel wasps?

This is powerfully argued and powerfully felt stuff, and I respect its honesty. This is where we may start to fear that delving too deeply here may endanger our faith. But God is always on the side of truth, so we must engage with truth, not hide from it. We must look the question posed by suffering and evil and the darker side of nature squarely in the face, with compassion, but without flinching, before we can come up with responses that are honest and real. Anything we say about suffering must not only be say-able to those who are really suffering, it must also be say-able, not so much to Stephen Fry himself, but to those who have those questions and accusations put to them and feel them deeply.

The answer (if it can be called that – though I don't think it can) of this book to the questions posed by suffering is that all this is 'because of love'. Because you and I and Stephen Fry are loved by God – that is why the world is as it is. But that will need some unpacking, which is what I want to do in these pages.

Chapter One – Phrasing the Question

The experience of suffering – our own, or even more in the case of those we love - can be where faith breaks. But, also, it is where it often reforms, because how does leaving faith behind *help*? That's an immediate response to the attacks of Fry and those like him. In what way does your approach help? How does giving up belief in a loving God make the existence of bone cancer and jewel wasps any better? If you're after an easy logical consistency, giving up faith may, at first glance, resolve a mental dilemma, but in terms of real life it just makes it all worse. It removes one of the few sources of comfort and one of the major historical motivations for combating suffering. It's also emotionally inconsistent. One of the things we tend to most admire in Fry is his impassioned anger at suffering. We feel we could easily share that anger at God. But, if there is no God, why be angry about it? Fry's position reminds me a little of C.S. Lewis's description of his pre-Christian self:

I maintained that God did not exist. I was also very angry with him for not existing. I was equally angry with him for creating a world.[1]

It's a position that, though it is eminently understandable, is thoroughly inconsistent. If we simply live in a random and meaningless universe then, as the philosopher David Hume pointed out in the 18th Century, long before the modern atheists climbed on his bandwagon, bone cancer and jewel wasps are just what you might expect. There *is* no intellectual problem. It's sad we have to live and die like this, but there's no reason to be angry about it. There's no reason to complain. But there is something deep in us that *does* complain. This is *not* OK! The Christian may look at the world as it is and be angry and revolted, just as Fry is. But the Christian has a *reason* to be angry. Fry does not, unless at some level he believes in the God to whom he directs his anger and complaint. If there is a loving God, things should not be this way and we cry out to that God and we wrestle with the question and the reality of suffering. The atheist has no reason to wrestle. If there is no God, well... intellectual dilemma resolved. The problem is removed. But suffering is always a problem whatever you believe or don't believe. No one can deny that atheists can be just as compassionate as any believer, and just as angry at suffering, but they are doing so from a standpoint of 2000 years of Christian culture. Their anger *depends* on a faith standpoint that says, 'things should not be this way'. But if they are right and we really do live in an uncaring universe, then things *should* be this way. Why, then, are they angry? Hating suffering... perfectly normal... but why anger? If the atheists win the argument and, as a culture, we give up belief in a loving creator, in a thousand years time suffering will still be there, but no one will be appalled and angry about it. But I think Fry is *right* to be angry. It is just that his intellectual response saws off the cultural and emotional branch on which he sits.

It's perhaps interesting to ask why suffering is often *not* a barrier to belief for those who really suffer. In Africa, for example, the question that feels so acute for us, doesn't seem to be a barrier to belief.[2] Is it because religion is one of the only comforts they have? We might say, after Karl Marx, that religion is 'the opium of the people', an emotional painkiller, the crutch of the needy, so we might expect religion to be more prevalent where suffering is more prevalent. But isn't that contradicting the whole argument that we can't believe in God because of the existence of suffering? Also, isn't it somewhat patronising of us in the 'wise' scientific

West to despise those 'gullible' believers? It would be better to consider the anthropological fact that our Western unbelief is culturally unusual, whereas suffering is universal. It remains the case that, for those who *really* suffer, their suffering is often less of a barrier to belief than it is for us who watch it with horror from a distance. Is there something to be learned here? Perhaps they are used to terrible suffering being a part of life, when we tend to be so insulated from it. For them, faith co-existing with suffering is normal. Faith is discovered and lived out in these situations. For us, by comparison, our faith is mostly born in situations of material blessing. When trouble comes we then question the reality of it. We also need to be careful not to be patronising to those who started the world faiths in the first place. It wasn't as if they hadn't thought of suffering! In fact, faith, in many, perhaps most cases, is largely a *response* to the existence of suffering in the world.

In many ways faith (particularly Christian faith) is a rebellion against the world as it is – or against the world as it is commonly perceived. It is all too true that the Church has often been part of the status quo, but that is not a Christian standpoint. Fry and others like him are spokespeople for what is becoming the current status quo – the default position that there is no God and that science can explain everything, so faith is at best unnecessary, at worst harmful. In this intellectual climate faith stands on the edge as a sort of resistance movement, saying something like, 'If the universe is an uncaring tyrant, is that a good reason for joining its side?' We feel that there is something wrong. There is a question to be answered.

Now while I can't claim to have experienced terrible suffering first hand, one personal event did bring the questions home for me. Eight years ago, we lost our second child, baby Hannah, who went full term but got tangled up in her umbilical cord and died in the womb a few days before she was due. At times of great personal tragedy some seem to lose their faith, and being familiar with the philosophical problem of suffering from an academic perspective, I suppose I always assumed I would understand that if the same happened to me; but it surprised me to find that quite the reverse was true. It may have been uncharitable, but at the time, rather than identifying with such people, my raw response was to lose patience with them. From my guts my first response was almost angry. "How dare you use the suffering or death of someone else – even if it is someone you love - to excuse yourself from wrestling with the mystery of the universe!?"

As I said, that was probably uncharitable, but it was my first thought. That emotion has moderated since, and I won't use my own experience to judge others who have gone through far worse trouble and found their belief more challenged than I did, and, who knows, something may yet happen to me that will challenge me more deeply. When I was in the midst of the raw emotion of the loss, though, my thought was that those who lose their faith because of suffering (theirs or another's) are either making excuses to leave behind the inconvenience and struggle of faith, or they simply don't believe in the same God I do. Or rather, I don't believe in the God they don't believe in either. Perhaps I was lucky, or just unusual, but my Christian faith, while wounded, felt unchanged. My conclusion was this: if you only ever believed in God because you thought you'd get some sort of protection from suffering, then that was probably just a superstition – like believing that touching wood really might help.

Not that faith doesn't make a difference. Many wrote in their cards to us at the time, that they were praying our faith would give us strength and comfort of some sort, and, for myself, I can say it did, though perhaps not the sort of comfort many expect. C.S. Lewis wrote in 'A Grief Observed' about his pain at the loss of his wife to cancer; *"Talk to me about the truth of religion and I'll listen gladly. Talk to me about the duty of religion and I'll listen submissively. But don't come talking to me about the consolations of religion or I shall suspect that you don't understand."*[3] *person or thing that consoles*

Belief in God really doesn't function like some sort of emotional painkiller – an 'opium of the people' – or a crutch when you've been crippled. If anything, I suspect it makes you feel things more keenly. That has been my own experience. Jesus said he came that we might have life – be *more* alive – not deadened to the pain of living. But I think the strength faith brought for me at that time was that it set everything – joy and pain - within an overarching Love that is not rendered meaningless even by apparently meaningless tragedies.

I suspect (actually I *know* from speaking to people) that many who give up faith because of suffering thought of it as some sort of deal with God. 'If I worship God, I'll get some sort of protection.' A sort of 'prosperity Gospel' is prevalent among many. But God hasn't stuck to his part of the deal, so we give up. But it doesn't take much thought to realize that, from a Christian perspective, this is a major misunderstanding. The one person who ought to have been more protected than anyone else, on this view, was Jesus, and look what happened to him.

The question of God and suffering is far more than just a logical one, but the problem for believers can be phrased in a logical way. It is irrational – logically inconsistent - claims the atheist, to believe in God, because you must hold inconsistent beliefs like:

13

1) God is all-powerful and can do whatever He (or She, if you prefer) likes,

2) God is perfectly good, and

3) Evil and suffering exist – which cannot be denied.

These three beliefs, it is claimed, can't be held together because Good is always opposed to Evil and will always eliminate it if it can – and if God is all-powerful, God can. This is sometimes called 'The Problem of Evil'. Personally, I find it disturbing that so many thinkers have been content with the idea of Good 'eliminating' everything opposed to it. It's a bit of a Hollywood attitude, where the 'good guys' are those who are ultimately better at violence than the bad and manage to 'eliminate' them. Is God like this? Eliminating those who do evil and cause suffering?

But surely some of the things we see in this world a good God *ought* to want to do something about? Couldn't an all-powerful God have just given the tiniest nudge to prevent a baby's bath seat from toppling? Are we to conclude then that God is either non-existent, or not all-powerful? These are some of the questions we can look to address as our exploration goes on.

But while there are ways of answering the purely logical problem, we don't usually feel that suffering is a matter of logic. It is not generally the logic of the situation that troubles us. As I've alluded to already, the 18th Century sceptical philosopher David Hume, put it like this:

Continue the same.

"However *consistent* the world may be, allowing certain suppositions and conjectures with the idea of such a Deity, it can never afford us an inference concerning his existence. The consistency is not absolutely denied, only the inference."[4]

Work out from evidence.

14

The existence of a good God may be logically consistent with the existence of evil and suffering, but given the horrors of the world, Hume argued, is it *likely*? You wouldn't, Hume argues, look at the random sufferings of this world and 'infer' (logically conclude) there was a good God behind it. Doesn't the state of the world count as evidence against, rather than for, God? Ultimately Hume's argument was, if the world is designed, it seems like a bit of a botched job! There are not just winds but hurricanes, not just rains but floods, and nature is 'red in tooth and claw'. In the words of a Levellers song from the 1990's, "Isn't Nature wonderful? ... But is this art?"[5] It is also a matter of the sheer *quantity* of suffering. We are talking, not about isolated cases, but about the lives of millions – not just now, but throughout history. My son is keen on the books and related BBC TV series, 'Horrible Histories'. Though it is often extremely funny, you don't have to watch that program for long to start wondering, 'What on earth was God thinking when he let us loose on this world!?'

But suffering is still far from just an intellectual problem – whether one of logic or of otherwise – about squaring how we feel about things with our religious beliefs. Ultimately evil and suffering are not intellectual problems – they are 'existential' problems – which is philosopher-speak for saying they must be *lived* with. It's not just about how we *understand* suffering – it is how we *live* in the face of it. It is not about *under*standing evil and disaster, it is about *with*standing them. It's not just about answering questions, but about how we carry on.

"For axioms in philosophy are not axioms until they are proved upon our pulses." John Keats

Chapter Two: No easy answers

So how do we go about framing a Christian response to suffering? From the very start, I cannot emphasise strongly enough that I don't think there *is* any answer to the intellectual question posed by suffering, but there is a good reason why there cannot be. Just think why you might *want* an intellectual answer to this question. Usually we want answers so we can fit things neatly into our world-view. The world clearly *isn't* neat, but we want a world-view that is! If we were able to find a simple intellectual answer (of the sort we usually seek) to the question of why there is suffering in the world, we would sit back and say (our minds satisfied by the neatness), "That's OK then." But evil and suffering, by definition, are that which is *not* OK! And God doesn't think they're OK either and God doesn't want us to have answers to why it's there and have us think it's OK that there is evil and pain. God wants us to feel it's *not* OK and wrestle with it and *do something* about it.

What use is an answer? If a child has been hurt, do you stand over them and explain to them the *reasons* why they are hurting?! How could that help?! They don't need answers, they need love. By extension you could say that is what we need as human beings living in this world with all its pain. We don't need answers. How could they help? What we need is love. The Christian faith believes that is precisely what we are given in Jesus Christ.

Some have argued against faith that, because giving an answer would be an unloving thing to do in the face of suffering, we should simply be silent about it. Job's comforters were helpful to him when they saw his pain and sat with him in silence (Job 2:11-13) but when they opened their mouths they became part of his problem. Some have said the practice of 'theodicy' as it has been called – the intellectual attempt to justify God in the face of the existence of evil and suffering – can only end up colluding with evil and suffering - saying it's OK when it's not, helping us rest content with the existence of evil and suffering as just part of God's will, instead of fighting against it.

I take the point of this, but sometimes we do need to have something to say. A refusal to answer because of possible collusion with evil and suffering is frankly not good enough. Sometimes those who suffer really *want* to know. They want some intellectual weapons for their fight. They *want* to explore. To refuse to try to answer can be far more cruel than clumsy attempts to answer that ultimately fail. When I think back to my angry emotions at those who give up faith when I was hurting, I think some of the root of that was an anger at those who give up faith to excuse themselves from engaging with the intellectual, emotional and existential struggle which is faith held in the midst of suffering. Though I don't believe there are or can be satisfying intellectual answers, it is still human to look for them. As Ludwig Wittgenstein once wrote, Philosophy doesn't necessarily have to make progress. It can be like scratching an itch.[1] Suffering is a place where we itch intellectually. That's part of being human. There may not be any answers, but to be human we must wrestle with this.

One who did was the 19th Century Russian novelist, Fyodor Dostoyevsky. He wrote a fantastic book called 'The Brothers Karamazov' (if you're going to read it, persevere – it has chapter after chapter of boredom, then flashes of absolute brilliance). Two of the main characters are the atheist intellectual Ivan and his little brother, the novice monk

Alyosha. There is a famous passage in which Ivan produces a devastating argument against God from the existence of suffering. The whole Chapter, called 'Rebellion,' contains the argument as Ivan elaborates on stories of suffering and cruelty he has come across, until he concludes with a question to his Christian brother:

"Tell me frankly, I appeal to you – answer me: imagine that it is you yourself who are erecting the edifice of human destiny with the aim of making men happy in the end, of giving them peace and contentment at last, but that to do that it is absolutely necessary, and indeed quite inevitable, to torture to death only one tiny creature, the little girl who beat her breast with her little fist, and to found the edifice on her unavenged tears – would you consent to be the architect on those conditions? Tell me and do not lie!"[2]

"No, I wouldn't," Alyosha said softly.

Ivan's question is unanswerable – and Alyosha has no answer. No amount of heaven in the end can ever make it all somehow 'worth it'. This is a challenge to a shallow reading of St Paul who said our present sufferings are not worth comparing with the glory that will be revealed in us.[3] Ivan cannot accept that. Even if there is a heaven he wants to return his ticket. It's not worth it.

Alyosha has no answer, but, I ask again, and I think Dostoevsky is asking in the novel, what *help* would giving up faith be? Atheists have liked to trot out Ivan's argument and point to it and the impossibility of answering it. What they don't tend to appreciate is that Dostoyevsky was a Christian – one who didn't get on too well with the established church, but a Christian nonetheless. The book goes on, and the impassioned Ivan slowly goes mad, while Alyosha quietly gets on with his faith – though he has no answers – and serves the poor and needy and does his best to relieve suffering, and he comes out as the quiet hero of the book.

Though from 150 years ago, this is similar to the conclusion of Philip Yancy's recent book, 'The Question that Never Goes Away: Why?' Yancy said, talking about his book;

"I've almost concluded you can answer the question "Where is God when it hurts?" with another question: "Where is the Church when it hurts?" When the Church is on the front line of suffering, people don't wave their fists at God. They know where God is – in God's people."[4]

Christian faith ought to be a motivation to help those who suffer and there are countless examples of the Church, despite its many human failings, doing this locally, nationally and internationally. It's not particularly important to a committed Christian to find answers to why there is suffering. It is vitally important to *do something about it*. Giving up faith because of suffering may appear to remove a logical inconsistency (but only at first glance), but it wouldn't help those who suffer one bit. It would remove one of the few comforts of those who do suffer and remove one of the major historical motivations towards helping those who suffer.

But even though I believe there are no answers, and there are good reasons why there are no answers; I'm not just going throw up my hands and say, 'It's a mystery!' and refuse to think about it. It *is* a mystery, but that's no excuse not to love the Lord your God with all your mind, as well as your heart, soul and strength. As Christians, I believe, we are called to be the people of God taking up the mantle of Jacob, who, after his encounter with the angel of the Lord in Genesis 32:22-32, had his name changed to 'Israel' which means 'He who wrestles with God'. To be a believer in this tradition is to be one who wrestles with God until it hurts. Faith is not a crutch. It sends us away limping. We don't have answers that allow us to say, 'That's OK, then!' because it isn't. As believers following in the tradition of Israel, we are called to be wrestlers with God, and wrestling with the question of suffering is no small part of this.

I don't believe there are answers that can be one hundred percent satisfying for the reasons I have given, but I do believe there are *some* things we can say.

Chapter Three - Because we're free

Our son, when aged 8, and having being asked whether he enjoyed a film he had watched, said he had, but complained it was a bit scary – scary and funny. He doesn't like 'scary' in films – his imagination is too strong. I found myself trying to explain that all the good stories are a bit scary and a bit funny. If nothing was ever scary, nobody would have to be brave. Then I realised what I had said. Perhaps that is one strand to why the world is as scary and horrible as it is? Not because it's more entertaining, but because if it was otherwise, much of what we value, like bravery and commitment and love and many other things, simply wouldn't be there. And particularly - it has been argued for centuries – without God's allowing suffering, we simply couldn't be free.

There is a fairly standard philosophical move in so-called 'theodicy' – the battle to justify God in the face of suffering. It is called the 'Free will defence', which sounds like some sort of gambit in chess, but basically it is the argument that God created a world in love, in the hope it would love him back, or at least that it would have love within itself. God has created and loves a world that produces creatures who will love God back and love one another in a reflection of God's love. But love, if it is to really *be* love, must be freely given – it has to be a real choice. No being can freely choose to love without also being able to freely choose *not* to love. The free choice not to love is pretty much what evil is, and a large proportion of the suffering in the world is caused by that choice. So, basically, evil and a large proportion of the world's suffering are the price we pay for freedom. They are the price we pay so that love can be real.

But what about sickness and disease and earthquakes and jewel wasps? These things are not 'evil' as such. They are not the products of a choice not to love. Sometimes Christians have said that these things too are the result of 'the Fall' – creation is somehow 'broken' by human sin and so these things result. This seems unlikely to me, as well as being a denial that the creation is good. In any case "it was God who made the Devil and the woman and the man and there wouldn't be an apple if it wasn't in the plan" as Sydney Carter said in his song, Friday Morning. We can't get God off the hook by saying suffering is all our fault, or even the Devil's fault – *even if it is*, because God made us and the Devil and everything. As creator, God bears ultimate responsibility. The buck stops there and can go no higher.

But the 'Free Will Defence' can be adapted to address this. It is not just human beings that are created to be free in an otherwise mechanically determined cosmos. It is the whole creation that is free – free to evolve and develop and produce creatures capable of love. The reason there are earthquakes and jewel wasps is that they are part of a free creation – free to develop its own way – made, in love, to produce free creatures that are capable of choice and love. This does not fully 'answer' the criticisms – there is still no answer. God is not off the hook as the buck for jewel wasps freely evolving still stops with him; but I think we can say that a God who creates a free cosmos does not necessarily directly will every detail of it into being. Stephen Fry is right that a God that carefully planned out a jewel wasp would be a bit sick, but a God that created a world capable of producing, by evolution, a creature as marvellous as Stephen Fry, even if it couldn't be done without all the other horrors of evolution, isn't quite so crazy. He is still ultimately 'to blame' if you want to put it that way, but natural 'evils' are a by-product, rather than something directly willed by God in every detail.

To put the question a bit differently; if you have a son who grows up to become an axe-murderer (heaven forbid!) are you to blame? Well that depends. Are you to blame because you brought him into the world? Most would say, probably not. If, by terrible parenting you twisted him into becoming a monster, then you would certainly bear some of the blame. But what if you were a perfect parent and gave him all the love anyone could ask for and he still went wrong? You may then still be the cause of his existence, but it would be a bit harsh to blame you for all his actions. The case is somewhat different for God of course, because He created not just individuals that go wrong, but a whole world that has 'gone wrong' in some ways. He created the very conditions for 'going wrong' in the first place. Also, the question might arise as to why God does not intervene to *stop* some of these goings wrong. Perhaps God does intervene in some cases, but then why doesn't he intervene in all of them? We'll come to that... but not answer it.

Freedom is, I believe, part of a Christian answer to why there is suffering; but only part of it. Ivan Karamazov's question still bites here. Is freedom worth it? Perhaps not, but a free world is the only world in which you or I or Stephen Fry or anyone else can exist. We may not like it and wish ourselves out of existence, crying out like Job that it would have been better if we had never been born (Job Chapter 3), but God ultimately disagrees. Your son or daughter may, in the depths of depression, think it were better if they had never been, but as a parent you would be unlikely to agree.

There are all sorts of holes that can be picked in the 'free will defence'. I don't think it ultimately works as an *answer* - but it's not a bad place to start. It does raise all sorts of other questions. One of which leads us on to our next chapter. If it is true, that the cosmos must be free to evolve and develop its own way in order to produce truly free creatures capable of love, and if it is true that a Creator God has let it go freely, to what extent is God 'in control' of creation?

Chapter Four - Is God in Control?

A common question that I come across as a parish priest caring for people who are going through the mill is, 'Why is God doing this to me?' 'What have I done to deserve this?' 'Am I being punished?' My knee jerk answer, which I believe is true, is, 'God *isn't* doing this to you?' While we may live in a world that God has allowed to go its own way, and this means we are subject to its random accidents, God doesn't deliberately and directly will the suffering of any of his creatures. As Jeremiah wrote in the book of Lamentations, "Although he causes grief, he will have compassion according to the abundance of his steadfast love; for *he does not willingly afflict or grieve anyone.*" (Lamentations 3:32-33)

But if God doesn't will this suffering to happen to us, and it *does* happen to us, then surely God isn't in control? Can He then be trusted? Is God worthy of our worship or is God simply powerless? To repeat the point slightly differently; *can* God intervene but chooses not to? But what would *we* be like if we could intervene to prevent a child drowning but didn't? Is such a God admirable? If God has chosen to limit his freedom for the sake of our freedom, is God then helpless? Is God *unable* to intervene? Is he then worthy of worship? And why do we pray to God to intervene?

To think of it as some sort of philosophical trade off (which I don't think is wise), it seems that to exonerate God from responsibility for evil and suffering we need to give up the idea that God is in control. Looking at the supposedly inconsistent beliefs we thought about in Chapter One (numbered 1 – 3 on page 14), we avoid the logical contradiction by denying the first of those beliefs. We might deny that 'God is all-powerful and can do whatever He likes' by saying God has voluntarily given up this power.

But is that what we want to say? If God has voluntarily given up his ability to do whatever he likes in his world in order that it might be free, the logical contradiction is removed, but is what we are left with recognisably the Christian God?

Can we talk of 'God the Father almighty' in the creeds if God cannot or will not do anything about suffering? What does 'almighty' mean if that is the case? This area needs a bit of thinking around if we are to frame a Christian response to suffering. The God of Deism – the 18th and 19th Century belief in a creator who had pretty much abandoned the creation to go its own way - might be easily logically consistent with the existence of suffering, but it is not easily reconcilable with the Christian God as revealed in the Bible and spoken of by Jesus.

So, what does 'almighty' mean in a Christian context, and can an almighty God be consistent with the existence of suffering? We could say that 'almighty' means simply that God's love triumphs in the end. Isn't that precisely what Jesus reveals? In Philippians Chapter 2, St Paul quotes a hymn to Christ saying that though Christ was in very nature God he did not consider equality with God as about grasping and controlling (Phil.2:6 - the Greek word is difficult to translate but I think this is a fair translation in this context). The God revealed in Christ chooses to empty Himself, and part of what that means is that he chooses to give up control. As a parent gives up control over a child's life, in order that they may grow and live and learn to love independently, so God gives up control over us, and, to some extent, over Creation as well. Particularly if God is most perfectly revealed upon the Cross, what does this say about God's almightiness and control? It can be strongly argued that a specifically *Christian* answer to any questions about the existence of suffering is bound to take this into account and therefore to raise a doubtful eyebrow at the idea that God is in control. At least it ought to question the idea that God's control extends to preventing suffering, even though it may be conquered via the Cross.

Also, doesn't a desire to control everything display weakness – not almightiness? As human beings we want to be in control because we are afraid we might not be able to cope with the consequences if we lose control and things we don't want to happen come about. The control freak is not a strong person, but a fearful one.

But if God isn't in control – if a certain amount of randomness has been built in to creation in order that freedom and love may exist - then creating is a terrible *risk*. But then giving life generally is. Conceiving a child is a risk – a sacrificial risk even – it will cost you (sometimes) 9 months of illness and may end in miscarriage or still-birth. Being blessed with so much medical care we sometimes lose sight of that risk. Occasionally I am asked to book a baptism for an as yet unborn child. Given what happened to us, that upsets me. I don't let on – I say 'congratulations' and do what we can to book the happy event – but it seems a terrible presumption to me. Creating life is a risky business. Creation is a risky business.

In our absurdly risk-averse culture we think that is somehow negligent of God. We would often prefer conception didn't happen at all than be exposed to all that risk. We would prefer *contra*ception (literally 'measures *against* conception') than let ourselves in for the roller-coaster ride. *We* probably wouldn't create in those circumstances – we would shut the risk out. But if you unpack that, what it is saying is we would rather not exist at all. Is that really what we want to say? Ivan Karamazov is almost literally saying that. He would rather we didn't exist at all than have some (particularly children) go through suffering. If that is really what you want to say there is not really an answer, but you are wishing yourself (and everyone else you love, including the children) out of existence. The choice doesn't seem to be between a better world and this one. It is between this one or no world at all – or at least a world in which we wouldn't exist.

It is a subject for a whole other book, but I find the kind of risk-averse culture which stops events and good things happening – prevents children playing because of risk, etc – the whole mindset that 'Health & Safety' has become – this is a *profoundly* anti-Christian concept. Our culture would rather nothing good happened at all than risk something bad happening, so many good things end up removed from our society because we can't cope with risk. As part of our modern mindset this may be no small reason as to why we find a God that *does* allow risk so difficult to believe in.

Existence itself is a scary thing. Some thinkers (like Friedrich Nietzsche) have written about 'the terror of existence'. Is this what a newborn child cries about? Be afraid – be very afraid – this is *Life* in all its wonder and terror. On balance, would we say the world is good? Is it *worth* it? Ivan Karamazov (and Stephen Fry it would seem) and those like him say, 'No!' (though it's interesting that the author who created Ivan does *not* say 'No'). If it were a mathematical equation it would be hard not to agree with him. But it *isn't* a mathematical equation. It's not about a balance of 'worth it' versus 'not worth it' – it's about *love*. It is 'because of love'. Why do parents bring children into the world? Some motives may be more problematic, but for the most part it is *because they want to love*. They just don't *care* that the world is a horrible place and all sorts of nasty things may happen to their child. We know our children are certain to see a lot of bad stuff come down in their lifetime. Some indeed don't have children because of just those sort of motives, but most just feel they *have* to bring life into the world. They want – they *need* – to love.

You could say that is just your genes wanting to reproduce themselves, but that's perfectly compatible with a world set up by a creator to produce life and love. Is it just instinct? Is it right to dismiss love in that way? It may be instinct but there's no 'just' about it. I suggest it is God's instinct to produce life in order to love. Does God *need* to love? I'm not sure we can say God 'needs' anything in the way that we do, but perhaps we can say he *chooses* to need to love. Is that, then, self-centred of God? He wants or needs to love so he throws us into the horrors of existence? But isn't that precisely the *reverse* of self-centredness? God could have had a perfectly happy and harmonious universe with only Him in it. But if you want a universe with love in it, this universe we have is what it looks like. We may wish it was otherwise, but that would be to wish ourselves out of existence.

At this point I'd just like to step back for a moment and say, 'Take care…' Is this a harsh thing to be saying to the mother of the child whose baby has drowned in the bath? There is a danger we could be saying something like, 'Like it or lump it!' That's why none of this thinking around the subject of suffering can be an answer. It doesn't stand up as an answer. Nothing does – for the reasons already given. Nothing can make it all right. But it is something that can be *said*.

We can say the existence of suffering is not fatal to belief in a loving God because a universe with love in it needs to be a universe free to go its own way; and while this is a risk that allows all sorts of terrible suffering to exist it also allows love to exist. Just as a parent steps back from controlling

29

their child in order that they may grow and develop and be free to love themselves, so God steps back from controlling the universe. Some level of randomness seems to be built in.

While this might help us speak gently about the problem of suffering, here we run into a tension with the Bible, which certainly seems to speak of a God who is in control. It also leads us into a tension with the normal Christian practice of prayer. Why pray for those who suffer if God can't or won't do anything about it? I am fully aware (before philosophers and theologians start jumping up and down!) that there may be other ways of looking at prayer than as a means of getting God to act in the world, but it's hard to get away from the fact that the 'normal' Christian practice of prayer would be difficult to sustain without some sense that God might be willing or able to answer those prayers.

The whole story of the Bible speaks of a God who is in control of the broad sweep of history. God called Abraham and revealed Himself to him. Abraham's descendants were brought out of Egypt by God's mighty hand and outstretched arm. When it all goes disastrously wrong and God's people are exiled to Babylon, this is not seen as a random accident, but as God's judgement on his people to teach them to find Him in exile before they can return. And the coming of Jesus is interpreted as prefigured and even predicted in all this history. This is the bigger picture, and, more specifically, you don't have to flick pages in the Bible for too long to find quotes that suggest God is in control. I won't engage in a Bible study of these here. Suffice it to say that if you find a quote that suggests God is in control and think it contradicts what I have said about a world with some randomness and freedom built in, I acknowledge the difficulty! Perhaps the verses can all be summed up in the frequently quoted, "... in all things

God works for the good of those that love him…" (Rom.8:28) How can he if he is not in control?

The more I think on this the less I think we can say God is not in control without it being a lack of trust. How can Jesus tell us not to be anxious (Matt.6:25-27)? If God isn't in some sort of ultimate control, the trust he advocates is misplaced, as is the trust of all Biblical figures.

Jesus himself says, "Are not two sparrows sold for a penny? Yet not one of them will fall to the ground apart from the will of your Father." (Matt.10:29) Although there are more subtle ways of interpreting these verses, this isn't the place for detailed biblical interpretation; but there does certainly seem to be a tension here between saying God has allowed a free world to go its own way and grow, and the sentiment behind these verses and the whole story of the Bible. Can it be resolved? Again, while I don't think satisfying neat answers and schemes are to be had, there are things that can be said.

Is God 'in control' of this world? I want to say both, 'yes' and, 'no'. 'No,' because I can't see how God can be in full control and not be arbitrary or cruel about who he helps and who he doesn't. If God is in control there are some pretty huge questions to answer. But I also want to say, 'Yes, God *is* in control in some way,' for otherwise isn't God helpless? And you would pretty much have to throw away large chunks of the Bible that firmly assume God is in control and able to intervene. And much of Christian prayer would cease if we didn't believe God could help those in need. Is it possible to say both, 'yes' and 'no' to the providence of God without being irrational or illogical or throwing your brain in the bin?

Can God be in control of the broad sweep of history without being in control of the smaller details? Personally, it has sometimes *felt* to me that God has been at work, even in some of the smaller details of my life as I look back in retrospect. How can God be both in control and not?

Richard Holloway in 'Dancing on the Edge' elaborates a metaphor I find helpful. Holloway says we have tended to think of God as the leader of a marching band, conducting every player and keeping them precisely to the musical score. God has often been seen as keeping history – in the broad sweep, and in our individual lives – to a precise script, but the world does not *feel* that way. But how about if we thought of God as the leader of a jazz band? Jazz, though it broadly knows where it is going and knows what tune it is playing, allows itself considerable freedom to improvise. The leader of the jazz band knows how to incorporate the different instruments freely doing their own thing, and is even able to incorporate the 'bum notes' into the overall scheme of the music.

Holloway is more interested in our moral responses but his thought can be applied more widely. Basically, he says that because we often like to stick to controlled scripts and scores, we assume God must be like that too. Holloway writes:

"If we can find the courage to abandon the text when necessary and improvise in response to the audience and its dialogue with us, we soon learn that we are making a new kind of music with people rather than forcing them to listen to the few tunes we have in our repertoire. This is the genius of jazz, and it requires not only courage in the performer but considerable musicianship as well. This kind of improvisation is pure music making, and in the history of art it must have come before notation and written composition, just as story-telling came before writing and oral tradition came before the production of texts…

… fear of departing from the text is in marked contrast to God's method in creation, which seems to be characterized by a genius for adaptation and improvisation. The picture of God which science gives us is more like a jazz player than the engineer of the Newtonian universe, with its fixed, mechanical laws and determinate purposes."[1]

Holloway is speaking about living this way in response to God, because this is what Creation is like. This is to live in accordance with the way the world is made. We should live in an improvising way, because that is what God has done in creation. It's not so much that God isn't in control, but God is improvising. There is risk in this, but it makes for a free creation and can say something about God being in control of the overall scheme and working even our 'bum notes' for good, and even the 'bum notes' of evolution can find their place. I also think Holloway has to be right that improvised music came long before anyone thought of keeping to a particular tune. God, as the musician of creation, is an improviser who, while He knows where the music is going, is not controlling everything in accordance with a detailed score.

Another image, which I think brings out the tension perfectly and, while not exactly resolving it, holds the tension beautifully, is portrayed in the 1994 film Forrest Gump. The image of a feather blowing on the wind runs through the film and it's summed up near the end as Forrest, who has what we might call severe learning difficulties, stands at the grave of his wife and he agonizes over the meaning of it all with the wisdom of simplicity:

"I don't know if Mama was right or if it... it's Lieutenant Dan. I don't know... if we each have a... destiny... or if we're all just floating around accidental-like on a breeze... but I... I think... maybe it's both. Maybe both get happening at the same time..."

On one level that's just a contradiction, but in my guts I feel there is something deeply true about it. It just seems to chime with life and experience. Sometimes the most chance encounters seem to be those that most shape our lives. And sometimes they seem to make so much sense that it's hard to dismiss them as accidents. Somehow God is in control *and* it's all 'accidental like'. Perhaps both are happening at the same time.

Is that having our philosophical cake and eating it? Perhaps, but maybe the cake's big enough for that! But there is a serious question here about logical contradiction. Can things really be genuinely accidental and out of God's control, and yet God also be in control of the whole thing? Some philosopher will argue that that's like saying you can have a square circle – just a logical contradiction – meaningless nonsense. But this reminds me of a university lecture I once attended – all of us young philosophers – and we were discussing logical contradiction and the square circle example came up. The lecturer said you can't even *imagine* a logical contradiction - not without fooling yourself. Is that what Forrest Gump is doing? He might *think* he can imagine both accident and destiny happening at the same time, but he can't really. A fellow student said in the lecture that he thought he could imagine a square circle. He was universally

34

mocked and the lecturer challenged him to draw a square circle. He did –
at least to his satisfaction – basically a square with very rounded corners.
He was laughed at (philosophers are not the kindest when their certainties
are challenged) – including by me, as we felt he didn't get the point, but
now I wonder... was he trying to make a deeper point that the rest of us
didn't get?

Obviously, you can't get a genuinely, perfectly geometrical square
circle, which is both a perfect circle and a perfect square. That *would* be a
logical contradiction. But the real world is not made up of perfect circles
and squares. It's not made up of perfect *anything*. Yes, you can imagine,
and even draw a square with rounded corners – with some imperfect
attributes of a circle – not a round square, but a rounded square. So can't
it be possible in life, which is much messier than basic geometry, that
accident and destiny can be muddled up together? As I said, my guts
(rather than the logical half of my brain) tell me that there's something
deeply right about that.

This also chimes in with Christian thought about the 'now and not
yet' of God's Kingdom. Even though we live in a world of imperfection and
suffering and tragedy, it is here we find God's Kingdom at work, breaking
through – God's future invading our present. This isn't linear or logical, but
it is something we do seem to experience. Often believing in 'the
Providence of God' is taken to consist of believing that God has a plan that
will come to pass, and so the future must be entirely fixed. After all, doesn't
Psalm 139 say, "Before a word is on my tongue you know it completely, O
Lord... All the days ordained for me were written in your book before one
of them came to be." (Ps.139:4,16) There is a question here about God's
foreknowledge and whether that impinges on our freedom. The debate is

complex, but to sum it up and cut many corners, I think if God sees all of history from beyond space and time in eternity, that doesn't have any more effect on our freedom than my observing your actions, as they happen, affects your freedom. A more rounded biblical picture seems to be that, while the ultimate victory of God and the reign of his Son is assured, and the earth will be filled with the glory of God as the waters cover the sea (Hab.2:14); we still have freedom to be involved in that or not. And in that freedom "it is God who works in you to will and act according to his good purpose." (Phil.2:13) God has a plan but it is not fixed in every detail. God's proclamation of future judgement can be changed by our repentance. See the whole story of Jonah, for example. God is pictured as changing his mind in response to our free decisions.

God is working his purpose out. In the bigger picture his purposes cannot be thwarted. The picture that seems to emerge is one of God, not micro-managing, but still in overall control. But sometimes it seems God does manage the detail as well. We can trust him for the little things like food and clothing, Jesus says. But that does lead back to the question of God's controlling the bad things, the lack of food and clothing, the tragedies? If not a sparrow falls to the ground apart from his will, what about children who get cancer or die in accidents, and what about where the earthquakes strike and when? The question does go round and round and keeps reforming. It is not an answer. Rather, here is the open wound of faith.

One final image to help us hold in tension these poles of God in overall control, but still allowing the world randomness and freedom because of love: John Lucas describes God's providential control using the image of rug-making in a Persian family, where the children learn the craft by weaving from one end of the rug, while the experienced father of the family weaves from the opposite end. The father takes into account whatever mistakes his children make, skilfully working the whole into a beautiful symmetrical pattern. In a similar way God makes something beautiful out of the whole, even though he isn't directly responsible for every stitch.[2]

To conclude, a specifically Christian response to the question posed by the existence of suffering, does not necessarily have to give up the idea that God is in control, though it is hard to escape the idea that some element of randomness and freedom must be part of creation. But if God has, or to the extent that God has, let go of control, it is because of love... because God is love.

Chapter Five - Some Responses in the Bible

I don't propose now to undertake a detailed Bible Study of every possibly relevant text. I would suggest, though, that the problem of suffering, far from being something the Biblical writers hadn't thought of – an oversight that threatens their belief system – is there in the minds of the writers, behind all they say. How could it not be? If these texts are honest responses to the mysteries of human existence they couldn't leave this out. Consequently, you could take pretty much any passage from the Bible and make some sort of reflection on the problem of evil and suffering. A book fully addressing this would therefore end up longer than the Bible itself by some considerable margin. But here are a few thoughts that I have found to be significant.

Job – The book of Job is written as a direct response to the questions posed for believers by the existence of suffering. It argues against the commonly held view, in its day as well as ours, that suffering is God's punishment, or that faith will somehow protect us from things going wrong.

Job never gets to know why he suffered and the book is not an attempt to 'answer' questions about suffering. It leaves suffering as an open wound, but it does do a lot of poetic and often 'religiously incorrect' wrestling. In the story, Job is actually portrayed as suffering *as a result* of his faith. The Satan – a sort of 'counsel for the prosecution' in the divine court – says Job is only faithful and good because God protects him from suffering. So, God allows (but does not directly cause or will) Job's sufferings. I don't think this little passage about the Satan is supposed to be an explanation of suffering in general; but is just a little speculative scene-setting to explain how God might be in control and yet the righteous might still suffer. It sets the scene that Job in no way *deserves* what happens to him.

To start with Job, though devastated and miserable, copes pretty well. He asks, why should we accept good things from God and not accept suffering? He calls his wife, who suggests he should curse God and die – give up his faith because of suffering, a 'foolish woman'! (Job 2:10) His friends come, and are so horrified by his state they can only sit with him in silence. In doing this they are perhaps of some comfort to him. But then they open their mouths and try to provide answers and this proves to be too much for Job, especially as they are basically arguing that God is just and in control, so Job must have done something to deserve this.

Job starts by wishing himself out of existence. It would be better if he had never been born. In a sense he sides with Ivan Karamazov – returning his ticket to heaven. And he accuses God of being unjust to him. His friends, their faith threatened, try to come up with answers and make matters worse. What follows is a debate in Hebrew poetry – the friends on one side and Job on the other. And when the friends fail to silence Job's complaint, a frustrated bystander called Elihu wades in as well. Job never gets quite as far as cursing God – in fact he says at one point, "Though he slay me, yet will I hope in him." (Job 13:15) – but God certainly gets an earful!

After all the debate – 35 chapters of poetry – we might expect some sort of answer to the question of suffering, but we don't get one. To our modern rational mindset, it all seems very unsatisfying. What Job does get is a response from God, who appears in a thunderstorm and speaks back in poetry – but he doesn't get an answer. God rebukes Job saying,

"Who is this that darkens my counsel with words without knowledge?" (38:2); though later he also rebukes the friends saying "you have not spoken of me what is right as my servant Job has." (42:7)

The response that Job gets is pretty much to tell him, 'You know nothing!' "Where were you when I laid the earth's foundation?" (38:4) You don't have the faintest idea of why there is suffering in the world. God draws Job's attention to the wonders and mysteries of the natural world. Creation is wild, untamed and exists for itself and cares nothing for us. We live in a world full of wild beauty but it is not geared to make our lives comfortable. The poetry is after, I believe, the feeling engendered by C.S. Lewis's description of Aslan. He's not safe, but he is good. This creation is not safe, but it is good. The bigger picture is revealed to be something way beyond the human mind to grasp. Job does not get answers. There *are* no answers. He is simply told his well-being is not the whole purpose of the universe, and that he is wrestling with things he cannot understand.

Though we might find it frustrating, I think the book of Job is wise not to attempt rational answers. It understands that they could only be shallow, whereas what we are dealing with is deep.

Psalm 23 – One of the best known (and oldest) passages of scripture is the 23rd Psalm. It speaks of the Lord being our shepherd; caring for us, leading us beside still waters into green pastures. When I read or sing these words at funerals, which I frequently do, I'm conscious of the tension. Most of the mourners don't feel they are beside still waters at that moment. But, of course, then we hear the words, 'When I walk through the valley of the shadow of death thou art with me, thy rod and thy staff they comfort me.' Our shepherd never said we wouldn't go through the valley of the shadow of death. There are some things he doesn't protect us from. But he does go there with us, and we experience his rod and his staff there. If God were simply sat on high, watching this world from a distance, telling us, 'You must go through this suffering because it is the cost of the existence of love,' that God would be a bit of a monster. But that is not the biblical picture of God. God is *with* us – God is 'Immanuel' (Hebrew for 'God with us'). This comes out even more sharply when we come to the New Testament when the Good Shepherd, named Immanuel at his birth, doesn't just follow and comfort us, but walks into death with us. "When you pass through the waters I will be with you." (Isaiah 43:2)

Jesus – In Chapter 6 we'll look at the difference Jesus' life, death and resurrection make to the question of suffering, but here I just want to look at a couple of things Jesus himself *said* about suffering. Again, he doesn't address the question in a rationalist way, seeking intellectual answers, but he does say a few things.

On one occasion Jesus was asked why a man was born blind. Was it because he sinned, or did his parents sin? (John 9:1-2) A possible question behind the question is asking, 'Isn't God unjust to inflict disability and suffering on a baby because of his parents' sins, because he can't have sinned himself before birth?!' But the lesson of Job has been ignored and still the default assumption is that suffering must be the result of sin. Jesus' response indicates that this is wrong-headed. "Neither this man nor his parents sinned, but this happened so that the work of God might be displayed in his life." (v.3) Is the 'work of God' referred to the miraculous healing that's about to take place? That's usually how this passage is read, but I think it's deeper than that, or Jesus' response would be meaningless beyond the context of this one incident. We might take Jesus' response to refer to any disability. This happened that the work of God might be revealed. Disability, and indeed suffering, can draw out responses of love and care that reveal God in the world, in a way that wouldn't happen if everyone was perfect, superhuman and independent of any need for care from others. God's glory is, in this way, far better revealed in our imperfect creation than it could be in one that included no disability or suffering.

In Luke 13:1-5 Jesus is again asked about suffering. His attention is drawn to an incident of Roman violence, where some Galilean pilgrims had been killed. He also brings in an incident of natural disaster when 18 people were killed when the Tower of Siloam collapsed. The two facets of the philosophical 'problem of evil' are suffering caused by human evil, and what might be called 'natural evil' caused by disease or disaster. Jesus sums them both up together and then flatly refuses to give an answer again! However, he does say, again, it is *not* because of sin. "Do you suppose these Galileans were worse sinners ... because they suffered in this way? I tell you, no!" But then he adds, "but unless you repent you too will all perish!" That shocks us!

What does he mean? In all honesty, I'm not sure, but, as with most of his words, they are probably spoken to make us think, rather than to leave us with a definitive answer. In the case of the Galileans it would make sense to say, "Unless you repent of your violent response to Roman oppression this is what will happen to you all," as, in fact it did when the Romans destroyed Jerusalem in AD70. But that wouldn't make much sense in speaking about the Tower of Siloam incident. It could be a way of saying that we all die in the end and will have to reckon with the judgement. In that case aren't these questions about suffering simply a distraction from our own need to repent and turn our lives around to face God. In practice I'd say that is often the case. People use the questions about suffering to deflect the challenge that faith might otherwise pose to their way of life. They think they don't have to engage with God because these questions remain unanswered. Perhaps Jesus is attacking that attitude and saying something like, 'How dare you use the suffering of others to excuse yourself from having to wrestle with God!' The question he is asked is being used as avoidance of repentance, and Jesus doesn't allow that.

There is another comment of Jesus that is perhaps relevant. When he is asked about the end times, and what will be the signs that they might be upon us, he tells his questioners to beware of that sort of thinking (Mark 13 and parallels). He says wars and other causes of suffering must happen. There will be earthquakes and famines, but these, he says, are the beginnings of birth-pains. He is generally supposed to be saying that the end times will get far worse than this, and that is certainly one way of hearing him. But we could also hear the positive in what he says. Birth pains lead eventually to joy (John 16:20-22). Is Jesus saying that the sufferings of this world are like the pains of childbirth – not something anyone enjoys or faces lightly, but something necessary to bringing forth a better world?

As a general answer to the question of suffering, this would be something Ivan Karamzov would disagree with. No greater joy could ever make all the horrors of suffering 'worth it'. The price is too high. But, I'm not sure Jesus is doing anything as simplistic as giving this as a rational answer to a question, but perhaps, as a thought, it may contribute to our overall understanding and response to suffering. On one level it has to be true. We know from our own experience that pain is far easier to bear if we know it's going to be over soon – especially if something good is going to come from it – childbirth being an obvious example. I wouldn't dare say to a woman actually in the process of child birth that it doesn't matter because it'll all be over soon. I'd expect a punch on the nose! But once you have the child in your arms you feel differently about the suffering you've been through.

There is a parallel to be drawn. Once the suffering is over, or once it is seen in the wider context of a new world being brought to birth, we can think about it differently. Ivan might counter that that is all very well with childbirth or having your tooth out, but the torture of children is of a different order. We cannot imagine anything making that 'alright' in the end. As a philosophical 'answer' to all the questions that arise because of evil and suffering this won't satisfy, but this is not what Jesus is trying to give.

The Gospels – Bracketing out the overall theology of Jesus' death and resurrection, which we'll look at in the next Chapter, the Gospel writers may still be saying other things about suffering than can be found specifically in the words of Jesus. I think this can be summed up in the words of the mockers when Jesus is on the cross. In Luke 23 we hear them comment, "let him save himself if he is the Christ of God." and "If you are the king of the Jews, save yourself!" One of the criminals cries, "Aren't you the Christ? Save yourself, and us!" They all assume that divine power and status should amount to an ability to avoid or prevent suffering. Translated to our modern thought patterns this could be seen as a sort of parody of the claim that if there is suffering it can't be true that there is a God. Those who reject faith because of suffering are portrayed to be like those who mocked Christ on the cross, saying, 'What good is *this*?! Save yourself and us from this suffering!' They expect that, if he has the character of God, that is what he will do. But one of the primary purposes of the Gospels is to show us that idea of God is wrong. God does not save us *from* the suffering, he saves us *through* it, and *in* it, and shares it with us. The crucifixion is seen by his foes as proof that God cannot be with Jesus - that he cannot be the Christ. But the Gospel writers are all saying the cross actually reveals the glory of God. God, as revealed on the cross doesn't magic suffering away, or miraculously find a way to dodge it, but tackles it head on.

They derided Jesus. If God is with him he can bring him down from the cross. If God is real he can intervene. But if God *had* intervened what could faith say to those for whom he doesn't? As it is, faith proclaims God is *here*. He's mixed in with it. He has borne it. Easter then becomes a possibility.

The faith born in the Gospels is not one that is somehow threatened when the existence of suffering is pointed out – as if it hadn't thought of it. It is a faith born in the first place from a very deep engagement with suffering.

St Paul – The greater part of the thinking about God and Christ found in the New Testament originates with St Paul. As stated at the beginning of the chapter, pretty much everything Paul writes could be taken as some sort of an engagement with the existence of suffering, so whole books could probably be written on this subject, but there is only space here for a few nuggets from the rich vein of his thought around this area.

Paul was a man very familiar with suffering. In fact, he is so familiar with it that he appears to have faced disparagement and criticism from those who assumed that if God was with him he ought to be more protected. That criticism seems to be behind the second letter to the Corinthians.[1] The letter wades into the theme straight away speaking of a God who comforts us in our troubles so we can comfort others in theirs. (2Cor.1:4) Paul goes so far as to boast in his sufferings. In Romans he goes so far as to *rejoice* in his sufferings saying "suffering produces perseverance, perseverance, character; and character, hope" (Rom.5:3) At times he seems to almost say that God gives us sufferings to do us good. There is a danger here that God could be seen as an abusive parent, battering his children into good behaviour. If bone cancer and genocide are discipline we could get easily to a pretty sick picture of God. There is a tradition that sees the world as a 'vale of soul-making'[2] with suffering as one of the tools God uses to perfect us. As a general idea this might have some mileage, but if each individual instance of suffering is measured against this idea you get quickly to an unpleasant picture of God.

Paul is, I think, usually more subtle that this. The letter to the Hebrews (possibly by Paul, but probably not) nearly strays into this sort of territory in chapter 12, speaking of suffering as God's discipline. If you push this into a systematic philosophical doctrine it is unpleasant. Arguably, though, the writer is simply advising his readers that this is a helpful way to think of your *own* hardships – particularly persecution because of your faith. I don't think the writer intended it to extend to the death of our loved ones by accident or disease! But if we can take from this the general idea that creation is as it is because God loves us, and ultimately wants to do us good, it can move us to a position of trusting God, even though we don't understand. But that doesn't mean we have to wince under every blow of life, believing that God is striking us and saying, 'This will do you good!'

It is from Paul we get the powerful poetic image of creation itself groaning in bondage to decay (Romans 8:18-27). This is not an image of a creation actively willed by God to be full of suffering, but of something imperfect, even damaged, incomplete – not a bodge job by an incompetent deity, but the only sort of world in which God's glory, and ours, can properly be experienced and come to perfection in the end.

"We have this treasure in jars of clay to show that this all-surpassing power is from God." (2Cor.4:7) In the midst of the mess of our lives God's work can be seen. We live in a world of clay, in which there are wonderful treasures. Perhaps that shows us that when the good stuff happens it is from God, because you wouldn't expect it in a world like this. There is a tradition of responding to the so-called 'Problem of Evil' by pointing out the 'Problem of Good.' Why is creation beautiful? Why is there so much love and care? More of that later. Yes, we are clay, but in this clay, we do see 'glory', expressed as the overcoming and transformation of suffering. Suffering and weakness open up the space for love that really costs – a space that would not be there if the world contained nothing that was difficult.

For Paul, the gospel – the 'good news' of a different world-order to the one we thought was in control - is about being 'in Christ.' The Christian life is about placing ourselves, through baptism, in a new world-order – not one in which there is no pain, but one where pain is faced with love and courage. Being 'in Christ' is not about escape or protection from trouble, but about sharing Jesus' sufferings, and dying and rising with him. To be 'in Christ' is central for Paul, but difficult to understand. Perhaps the best way

I can think of it is to literally imagine myself living my life and worshipping God inside Jesus' suffering body. Medieval architects took this seriously. Churches and cathedrals were often cross-shaped, and one reason for this was for the worshipper to imagine themselves 'in Christ' on the cross. In some places (like Ripon cathedral) the sanctuary area was even built at a slight angle to the main body of the building, recalling Jesus head tilted to one side. They imagined themselves worshipping inside his body on the cross. Then, sharing his sufferings, they looked to share his resurrection too. Paul uses this image a lot. "We always carry around in our body the death of Jesus, so that the life of Jesus may be revealed in our body." (2 Cor.4:5) "... we share in his sufferings in order that we may also share in his glory." (Rom.8:17) Being a Christian doesn't mean protection from suffering, but often means shame and humiliation in the eyes of the world, but in this we find ourselves reflecting the true glory of God. The true glory of God is found in the face of Jesus Christ who went to Calvary.

Paul has obviously thought about this a lot. "While we live we are always being given up to death for Jesus' sake, so that the life of Jesus may be made visible in our mortal flesh." (2Cor.4:11) When our sufferings are brought to Christ they are transformed so that, though we are not immune to them, his resurrection is made manifest in our lives. The glory of God is found, not in the absence of suffering, but it is manifest precisely *in* the suffering and in the way it is transformed in the lives of those who are 'in Christ'. The life of Jesus is made visible in the world.

"Our sufferings are not worth comparing with the glory that will be revealed in us." (Rom.8:18) This is usually taken to mean that some future heavenly glory will ultimately compensate for all we have to go through on earth. As I said before, this would struggle against Ivan Karamazov's question which asks how the suffering of children can possibly be 'worth it'. But taken in context, Paul is being more subtle than this. It's more likely to be speaking about the glory that will be shown to the world in and through our sufferings, if we are in Christ.

There's no denying that Paul's attitude is radically different from our normal ways of thinking and reacting, and it can be a bit difficult to swallow. He suggests we ought to be thankful in our sufferings – even thankful *for* them. We tend to be thankful if the suffering is over or we have managed to avoid it. We give thanks if we are saved *from* suffering. But Paul is suggesting that we might be thankful because we experience the power of Jesus' resurrection *in* the suffering and difficulty. Paul is as aware as any atheist complaining about the existence of suffering that we *can't* see this. But we are called to look at what cannot be seen. Suffering produces *hope*, he says (Rom.5:3-4), but we cannot yet see that hope. Who hopes for what he already has? (Rom.8:24) Again, we might ponder that if creation were perfect there would be no need for hope... or faith... or love.

Not that Paul was content with the world as it is. He was not sat in a neat philosophical position that allowed him to say, 'It's all OK. It's OK there is suffering.' He wrestled intellectually and personally. He didn't seem to particularly rejoice in his famed 'thorn in the flesh' but desperately prayed that it would be taken from him. But, in the end, he concluded, not particularly that God wanted him to suffer whatever it was - indeed he saw it as a messenger of Satan - but that, in it, God's grace was sufficient, for God's power is made perfect in weakness. (2Cor.7-10) This would not be possible if we were all untroubled super-beings.

St Paul wrestled with Jesus as the image and glory of God, but even Jesus was not an untroubled super-being, but suffered a humiliating death

49

at the hands of the powers of this world. So, God cannot be a blown up version of earthly power and control. Rather he is revealed in suffering, thereby radically undermining the claims of the powers of this world to be divinely ordained. To pronounce Paul's early declaration of faith, 'Jesus is Lord' (rom.10:9) in parody of, and opposition to, the Roman declaration 'Caesar is Lord' is not to say that Jesus sits enthroned in all the trappings of earthly power, or that God is to be conceived of as a power like Caesar, only much greater. Rather it is to say that the title of 'Lord' belongs elsewhere – far removed from where we normally look for it. We look up and miss it, but if we look down we will find it washing our feet. God's sovereign power is displayed precisely within human weakness and suffering, and in loving response to it, not in the ability to avoid or inflict suffering.

Isaiah's Suffering Servant - To sum up this chapter, one final look back into the Old Testament, in case we are tempted to think this view of suffering – so radically different to the usual human ways of thinking - was a Christian idea, grown purely from reflection on what happened to Jesus and many members of the early church. It did grow from that reflection, but the early Christians believed it was solidly prefigured in the Old Testament. You do find debate and difference of opinion in the Old Testament. The book of Proverbs in particular seems to see prosperity and comfort as the rewards of God, and suffering and poverty as punishment for laziness or foolishness; but other so-called 'Wisdom literature', like the books of Job or Ecclesiastes take quite a different view.

The bigger picture of the Old Testament, taken as a whole, portrays it as part of the vocation of God's people to struggle and even to suffer, so that God's love might be revealed in the world. Abraham was called to be a homeless nomad, Jacob was called to be Israel – 'he who struggles with God', God's people were allowed to be oppressed that they might call out to God and be rescued. All of this seems to be summed up by the enigmatic figure of 'the Servant of God' in Isaiah.[3] This figure has caused a lot of controversy. Christians see it as obviously pre-figuring Jesus. Jews see it as a figure representing the people of Israel as a whole. Both are, I think, right, because it seems that Jesus saw his calling to be this Servant, representing Israel as a whole and bringing to completion the calling God had always had for his people – to be a light to all nations by revealing God's glory in suffering and dying and coming out the other side victorious. Isaiah 52:13-53:12 in particular portrays the servant of God as a man of sorrows and familiar with suffering. Again, a radical departure from the idea that being faithful to God is supposed to protect you from pain, but rather, "it was the Lord's will to crush him and cause him to suffer" (Isa.53:10). This seems pretty dark, and a possible argument against all I have already said about God not directly willing suffering, until you bring in the specifically Christian idea that God himself was suffering in the suffering of the servant. It was the Lord's will to be crushed *himself* in order to bring about a far deeper healing. This is not simple masochism, but a familiar aspect of love. If those you love suffer, you would wish the suffering on yourself in order to help them. It is 'God's will to crush him' – and to be crushed himself – because of love. By his wounds we are healed. This leads us on to the next Chapter where we'll skim through what on earth Christian faith thinks was going on in the life, death and resurrection of Jesus Christ, because this is central to any Christian response to suffering. In fact, it is central to the Christian response to life in general.

Chapter 6 – Christmas and Easter and where they lead us

The two great festivals of the Christian year celebrate a God who is not a blown-up version of human power and strength, but a God who became 'little weak and helpless' and bore our weaknesses to the end, even sharing death with us. This is a very different idea of God to that which most non-believers *think* Christians believe in.

Atheists assume we believe in a God of power, like the pagan Zeus or Jupiter, and rightly point out that a god presiding over the world in that way seems to have not done a very good job. But Christians don't believe in the god the atheists don't believe in!

As an aside, I do wish the various celebrity atheists that spout about religion being nonsense would take a moment to understand what it is they are attacking. So often they waste their breath because they attack a form of belief that the vast majority of believers don't have. I wouldn't presume to tell a particle physicist that Dark Matter is nonsense; even though I think it probably is and they're barking up the wrong tree in looking for new particles to explain the missing mass of the universe. But as soon as I've said that, I know that actually I don't have a clue what I'm talking about, and those physicists are far more likely than I am to be right about this. And yet atheists who have never been to church, or certainly never seriously tried, as adults, to live Christian lives, think they know enough about religion to dismiss it. Just because they may have had experience of a fundamentalist rant at some point doesn't give them the right to tell me I'm stupid for believing all sorts of nonsense that I don't believe at all. They have every right to criticize religion (God can take it!) but I do wish they'd make some attempt to understand what they're criticizing. If I seriously want to understand the Dark Matter issue, I need to do more than read a couple of popular science writers before I think I can justly criticize those who live and breathe physics.

As I said, most Christians just don't believe in the god the atheists don't believe in. Indeed, in the ancient world Christians were considered to be 'atheists' by those who believed in the pagan deities, conceived as human abilities writ large on the sky. For those for whom religion was about ingratiating yourself with powerful spiritual forces, Christianity was seen as foolishness. (1 Cor.1:18-25) Why believe in a God who suffers? What good is *that*?! Where's the strength in becoming weak? But, from the earliest days, Christians proclaimed at their baptisms (and still do) 'I am not ashamed of that idea.' As they are baptized Christians are charged, "Do not be ashamed to confess the faith of Christ crucified." That is the whole *point*! We worship a God who was prepared to empty Himself of divine power and control because of love, and even to enter in to our weakness and suffering.

At Christmas, Christians reflect particularly on the 'Incarnation' – the 'enfleshment' of God in the human being, Jesus of Nazareth – the idea that the Word of God – all that God wants to say - became flesh and lived among us and we have seen his glory (John 1). The New Testament speaks of Jesus as the image of the invisible God (Col.1:15), the exact representation of God's being (Heb.1:3). For Christians, if you want to know what God is like in terms we can understand, then look at Jesus. As a theologian would say, Jesus is the 'revelation' of what God is like.

But if this is true, what exactly does he reveal about God? How does Jesus' suffering and death square with the belief in 'God Almighty'? We thought about this at some length in Chapter Four, exploring whether

53

God is 'in control' of creation. If Jesus really is the incarnation of God, that would back up what we said there. The God revealed in Jesus is a God who, while he may be in ultimate control, doesn't exercise that control in the way human powers and governments do. Rather we find a God getting his hands dirty - taking the role of a servant - even to the extent of suffering with us – beside us, and even in us.

For much of Christian history God was thought of as unchanging, standing outside the realm of human pain, and therefore 'impassible' – which means 'immune to suffering'. If God could suffer that would seem to threaten the idea that God was at peace and those who were with God were at peace. The Council of Chalcedon (451AD) declared as "vain babblings" the idea that the divine nature could suffer, and it condemned those who believed it. But the Council's thinking about God did not come from the Bible but from ancient Greek philosophy; though it was normal Christian belief until very recently, historically speaking. Arguably it was the horrors of the First World War that broke the hold of this idea. Geoffrey Studdert Kennedy, the trench chaplain known as 'Woodbine Willie', felt this deeply and his poems were influential for many in smashing this idea of a God at peace in heaven while we suffer below. The second poem in his collection, 'The Unutterable Beauty', actually entitled 'The Suffering God' says;

> Are there no tears in the heart of the Eternal?
> Is there no pain to pierce the soul of God?
> The must he be a fiend of Hell infernal,
> Beating the earth to pieces with his rod.[1]

A God who could sit peacefully in heaven, having ordained the world to be as it is, not feeling it Himself, would not be worthy of worship. In his classic, if somewhat 'heavy', work of theology, 'The Crucified God', Jűrgen Moltmann brought the idea of a God who suffers into the mainstream of Christian thinking. His reflections grew from his own experiences of the Second World War and from thinking about the Holocaust, which is another historical reality that has changed the way believers think of God. Moltmann relates Elie Wiesel's account of being made to witness a hanging in a concentration camp where a youth dangled a long time, struggling, before the end. Wiesel heard someone behind him asking, 'Where is God? Where is he?' Wiesel's answer was, 'He is hanging there on the gallows.' Any other answer, Moltmann says, would be blasphemy.[2] It would lead to believing in a God who doesn't care, and lead to us not caring ourselves. Moltmann might be misrepresenting what Wiesel meant a bit. For Wiesel, at that moment, his God seemed to be dying with the hanging youth. But in another way, this strengthens the whole point. What we are speaking of in Jesus is a God who is capable, not only of suffering, but also of dying, with all the paradox and mystery that opens up.

It is this one thought, that God shares our suffering, that keeps me, personally, a Christian rather than a Jew or Muslim or any other sort of believer. While I respect and admire those faiths for many reasons, how they manage to answer the questions posed by suffering without recourse to a God who shares that pain, I cannot comprehend. The idea of a God who suffers is a very Christian one, and it comes directly from Christmas and Easter - the doctrine of the incarnation coupled with what happened on the Cross. But, as I said, as a commonly held belief it is relatively recent.

55

Though the newness of this belief is a fact, that does puzzle me a bit, because at least since the First letter of John in the New Testament, Christians have believed that God is Love. (1 John 4:8) Love isn't something God just does; it is central to God's very being. That is why creation is as it is; because of, and only because of, love. But if God does not suffer how can God love *at all*, let alone *be* love? If someone you love suffers, you suffer. That is pretty central to what love is. It would be inhuman – incomprehensible to us – to be able to serenely and peacefully love from a distance while the one we loved underwent any sort of pain. But that is what classical theology has held for centuries. No wonder we have struggled with the question of suffering! A God who couldn't feel our pain, couldn't be described as loving us in any way we could understand – or any way that we could accept as meaningful at all.

But if God is love and if love entails suffering, this suffering must run pretty deep in the being of God. You can see why classical believers were disturbed by this idea. If the Cross reveals that God suffers, this is not just a one-off event at Calvary, where God tasted suffering once. What Jesus underwent was pretty terrible by most standards, but we could imagine worse suffering. And it was all over in a few hours. But the Cross, while it is a once for all time event, is of eternal significance because it is also a window into the heart of God. God has no beginning and no end, so if what happened to Jesus brings suffering into the heart of God, that suffering has no beginning and no end.

And there are two sides to this coin of God's suffering. If you love someone and they suffer, your love leads you to sympathize and empathize so much that it becomes suffering for you as well. But you don't actually, physically feel what they're going through, though in many ways you sort of want to. You want to take it onto yourself for their sakes - to take it away if possible. Well if God is love, God wants to as well. But the difference between God's love and ours is God *can* take the suffering of those he loves on to himself. God not only sympathizes with our pain. God actually feels it. According to much Christian thought, our very existence is a participation in God's existence. Our very consciousness is a participation in the consciousness of God. All this leads towards the idea that God doesn't just suffer what Jesus suffered. What Jesus suffered reveals that God suffers *all* our suffering. God feels it all.

But how far do you take that? Does God feel the suffering of the cockroach attacked by a Jewel Wasp? There might be a serious question about whether the cockroach is conscious and therefore whether it does actually suffer, but forget that for now. *If* the cockroach suffers, does God share that suffering? If Easter is a window into the heart of God, is Christmas a window as well? How far does the incarnation go? Is the incarnation also a window? That might sound a bit crazy or mind-boggling but it has been seriously argued, by thinkers like Teilhard de Chardin, that through the incarnation of Christ, God is actually incarnate in all creation. Because of the one special incarnation, God is also present in and through all creation. We're getting into deep theological and philosophical waters here, that could lead us into using words like Pantheism (meaning 'everything is God') or Panentheism ('meaning everything is in God'), and losing most readers in a philosophical morass, trying to fathom the very nature of God. Having had a walk or two into this area, I don't recommend it as territory for most Christians to venture into. We quickly find ourselves using long words and thinking we understand them, when really, we're dealing with a mystery and trying to stretch language and thought beyond where it can meaningfully apply. There are some things we really can't understand. In any case, this is taking us away from our point. But, while this area is way beyond the scope of this book, it's still perhaps worth asking ourselves the question of how deep the incarnation goes. Does God feel *all* the suffering in creation? The answer will be tied up with how much we think God loves all of creation.

But there's a good reason why Christian thinkers down the ages rejected the idea that God suffers. Doesn't that just extend suffering for all eternity? Doesn't it simply double the suffering in the universe if God suffers it all as well? What good does God's suffering do? Jesus wouldn't be a Saviour if he just suffered and died beside us, in the same mess as us. Good Friday cannot be the end of the story. At Easter Christ rises out of the mess again and takes us with him. If God's suffering is part of the eternal nature of God, then so is this victory. If the Cross is a window into the heart of God, so is the Empty Tomb. The victory also has no beginning and no end.

The book of Revelation at the end of the Bible, paints pictures of mysteries we couldn't possibly comprehend. But it speaks of the Lamb, victorious and sharing the throne of God, yet looking as if it had been slain – the wounds and the suffering are there (Rev.5:6). "Those wounds, yet visible above in beauty glorified," as the hymn 'Crown Him with Many Crowns' has it. It's not, as Ivan Karamazov might complain, that somehow everything has been made 'alright' in the end, and that makes it all worth it. This is not to make light of suffering. One of the best 'explanations,' if you can call it that, of this can, I think, be found in Pierro della Francesca's fresco of the resurrection. Look at the picture (I'm sure you'll find it on some internet search engine easily enough) and look at the face of Christ.

There is no easy triumphalism there. No smile. There is an incredible expression that carries into the victory of the resurrection all that he has gone through on the cross and, in medieval thought, in his descent into hell. Jesus carries that suffering with him. The wounds as well as the victory are now part of the eternal nature of God. This is what you get if you combine Christmas and Easter - the incarnation and Jesus' death and resurrection. This is at the heart of Christian belief about suffering.

So, summing all this up, does God just sit up there watching the pain of the world saying, "Go through it all because I love you! It'll all be worth it. You can't see that yet, but trust me."? Wouldn't such a God be a monster – a fiend of Hell infernal? I think He would, if he didn't feel every bit of it Himself. But isn't that just what the Christian faith says? If Jesus Christ is the revelation of God, what sort of God does He reveal? An all-powerful controlling ruler? No. If the Cross is a window into the heart of God it shows us that God shares all this suffering – not just on one occasion 2000 years ago, but God feels *all* of it – far more keenly than we do. If you love and you see someone you love suffer that hurts you in direct proportion to how much you love. What if your love were infinite?

> Love's hard as nails,
>   Love is nails:
> Blunt, thick, hammered through
> The medial nerves of One
> Who, having made us, knew
> The thing He had done,
> Seeing (with all that is)
> Our cross, and His.   C.S. Lewis[3]

Chapter 7 - Because of Love

So, to start to conclude all the thought of this book so far... There are no completely satisfying answers to the questions raised by suffering. If God were just sat, holy and removed from our pain, saying, "You can't have answers, but trust me as I watch you go through all this." I'm not sure I could respect that God. But if God were to say, "You can't have answers, but trust me as I hold your hand and go through it all *with* you..." Well, that God I'm willing to trust. I may not have answers, but enough has been *said*, so that I can trust. I can still live in faith.

So, to start to wind up where we started ... What is it we *want* from an intellectual answer to the question about why a benevolent God would allow suffering? If we're wanting to rest comfortably with a neat answer, that is not going to happen and for good reason. Partly because that would simply be an inappropriate response to the existence of suffering – a response that God could not possibly desire for us. But also, it is because, if God is in any sort of control, there *are* some big questions to answer - charges to be brought even. This leads us to feel we need to justify God – to defend God. Sometimes believers can be too defensive. Disturbed by the attacks of atheists and our own doubts, we find ourselves trying to justify God – to absolve God of responsibility for evil and suffering – to get God 'off the hook'. But if Jesus is, as Christians believe, 'the Word of God' – what God wants to say to us - then, in Him, God makes no *attempt* to justify Himself with intellectual answers. In Jesus we see no attempt to get God off the hook. We don't get those sorts of answers. God has no desire to get Himself off the hook. Instead what we get is God taking full responsibility, and accepting the consequences Himself – we see God *on* the hook.[1] We see God engaging with this suffering world, to reveal to it the love for which it exists, and working to heal its pain.

This idea of attempting to justify God reminds me of Elie Wiesel's play, 'The Trial of God'. When it was adapted in 2008 as a BBC/WGBH Boston television play, it was dramatized, after Wiesel's own experiences, as taking place in a concentration camp, though Wiesel set his play in the Seventeenth Century. The questions, though, are universal throughout history. It could have been set in any time and place. The idea behind the play is that God has questions to answer in allowing suffering in his creation. The Jewish protagonists in the play put God on trial. They convene a court, with witnesses for the prosecution, arguing that God is culpable for allowing the existence of suffering – particularly the massacre of innocents – in His world. The defence try to get God 'off the hook', but the trial concludes that God is guilty. However, at the end, those who have been taking part in the trial go on to pray. What else do you do? Giving up prayer, the protagonists seem to conclude, wouldn't help anything. As human beings we have to respond *somehow* and prayer seems the only appropriate response, even for those who struggle to believe.

We are dealing with something we cannot answer. We are dealing with a mystery. We *don't* understand. I hope I haven't given the impression that I think I do! I feel like Ebeneezer Scrooge trying to work out what's happening to him in 'A Christmas Carol';

"Every time he resolved within himself, after mature enquiry, that it was all a dream, his mind flew back again, like a strong spring released, to its first position, and presented the same problem to be worked all through,"[2]

Every time we work through the questions we find we cannot come to a place where we feel this is all OK. It is not. Even God does not believe it is all OK. But it *is* good. I don't mean that suffering is good, but that we can still affirm that life is a good thing. This universe is a good thing. But we come to a place in the end where we conclude, with the prophet Isaiah, that, as the heavens are higher than the earth, God's ways are higher than our ways and God's thoughts are of a different order altogether to our thoughts. (Isaiah 55:8-9) It's not just that God is cleverer than us, in a human way, and if we just tried harder we could work it out. This is a different order of truth altogether.

Like those in Wiesel's trial, believers don't come up with answers, but we do carry on believing nonetheless. How is it better if you stop believing? What does that solve? It simply removes one of the few ways we have of dealing with suffering – psychologically, and as a motivation for doing something about it.

God is there in the suffering, *and* in the *response* that suffering evokes. After the Boxing Day tsunami of 2004 the then Archbishop of Canterbury Rowan Williams was asked, 'Where was God?'

"In response to the question, 'Where is God in all this?' I have two things to say... that God is the crucified one, the one who is in the midst of the pain not separate from it, secondly, God is to be found in the hands of those who are helping to bury the dead, to bring clean water to the living, to administer medicine to the ill and counsel to those in darkness. This is the faith of the church."[3]

God feels the pain Himself. That's where God is. In those who suffer. But not *just* there. God is also in the response to suffering. God is there wherever there is love.

My short answer to why there is suffering is, 'Because of love.' But this is not love in the abstract. It is not some immense, but rather vague tender feeling that God has for all the universe - a love so huge, how could it possibly care for the individual? But, I want to say to every reader, to everyone to whom I am privileged to minister, to *everyone*; there is suffering because God loves *you*... Yes, *you*! And each and every one of us... as the unique individuals we are... you and I and Stephen Fry.

I prefer to start and end with what I believe above all else, and that is that *God is love* so love *must* be the answer to everything. Even to the question, 'Why is there evil and suffering?' Because God loves us – all of us – every one of us – just as we are; and if the world was different we wouldn't exist just as we are. In fact, most of us probably wouldn't exist at all. If you've heard anything about Chaos or Complexity theory you will know that if you change one small parameter in a large-scale complex system, you change pretty much everything. The unpredictability of the weather is a frequently referred-to instance of this. The classic, if perhaps somewhat exaggerated, example says that if a butterfly flaps its wings over Beijing today you might get rain instead of sunshine in Scarborough in 6 months' time. We think we can imagine a world just like this one, just without suffering. And if we can imagine it, why can't God create it? But the reality is that if you change one small thing in this world, everything might be *very* different.

I will throw in a couple of personal examples to explain what I mean. My wife's mother was married to her first husband for some years before he died of cancer. She remarried and had another child - my wife. If cancer had been removed from the world, my wife, who I love, and who God loves, would not exist. And my children, who God loves, would not exist. And any grandchildren, or any other descendants we might have would never exist. So why is there cancer in the world? Because in a world without it, countless people who God wants to love would not, and could not, exist. Probably none of us would exist exactly as we are. So, there is cancer because God loves us! That sounds odd, but I suspect something very like it is true. The world needs to be as it is for *us* – the unique individuals we are - to exist, and God loves *us*. That doesn't mean for one moment that God *likes* cancer, or we shouldn't seek to cure it. It just says something about why the world might be allowed to evolve, by a good God, the way it has.

In 2009 we lost our baby, to one of those random accidents that just happen. Why couldn't God intervene in that? There is no answer. But I do know this... If she had lived we almost certainly wouldn't have had our third child – and God loves him too. In a world without random tragic accidents he wouldn't exist, and neither would most of us.

I don't personally think God sits up there controlling all that we see in this world. I think he has refused to control every detail, for the sake of love. If, in our simple human relationships, it is wrong – even abusive – to try to control those we profess to love – why can't we accept that something like that might be true of God in God's love for creation?

Why is there suffering? There is no answer because giving answers in the face of suffering is not an appropriate response. Trying to come to a comfortable intellectual position in an uncomfortable world would be some form of delusion. That's ultimately why I reject an atheist position that thinks it sits in a more comfortable place – more 'compatible' with a world of suffering. I don't *want* to be compatible with suffering! I don't want to find a comfortable intellectual position. I don't want to be intellectually lazy, or believe something that is demonstrably nonsense when it is measured against the world; but I would rather embrace the intellectual discomfort of holding faith in tension with suffering, than give up and come to some sort of intellectual rest.

But while there can be no comfortable answers, there are many things we can say (or there would have been no point in writing this book!). There are many partial responses that can make a Christian faith in a God of love a perfectly rational thing. We can speak about free will being a necessary part of the creation. We can speak about God giving up control to allow love the space to be. We can look at Jesus of Nazareth and speak of God 'on the hook'. But faith is not just rational. Reason can only take us so far. However, we can admit that without throwing our brains in the bin. Faith may be more than rational, but it is not less.

Christian faith says that God is love. If this is true, there is suffering because of love.

Chapter 8 - It's better than that!

Love is a joyful thing. We could, after a lot of reflection on the darker side of things, come to a grudging conclusion. "OK," we might think, "the existence of a good God is compatible with existence of suffering, but it's still a pretty miserable existence." But it can be better than that. God is Love, and love is a joyful thing. Reading all that has gone before in this book, we could come away with an image of God sharing all our suffering and sorrow, which I think is vital to a true Christian belief in God; but it could also seem that God's existence is made unhappy by ours. But God also shares our joy. God rejoices in all He has made, much as parents rejoice in their children. Sharing and feeling their sorrows, or being saddened by their failures and sins, does not preclude rejoicing in their happiness, enthusiasm, love and trust. In fact, the two usually go together.

Henri Nouwen, in 'The Return of the Prodigal Son' points out Jesus' teaching that God rejoices, not that the problems of the world have been solved, or that human suffering has come to an end, or that thousands have been converted, but God rejoices because *one* of his children who was lost has been found.[1] God is concerned for individuals, because love is concerned for individuals. God's love and joy relate to countless millions of individuals. We don't tend to rejoice in little things. We're used to hearing of huge and insoluble problems in the news – wars, violence, crime, disaster. We become accustomed to living with sadness at these things, and we see the world as a glass more than half empty of joy and meaning. But whenever I have spoken to folk who have lived and worked in places of great violence or poverty they (like the friend Nouwen describes[2]) don't speak primarily of the suffering they have seen, but about the comparative joy of the folk they have met and lived among. They speak of how ordinary people seem to hold faith and rejoice in circumstances where we imagine they would be miserable. This isn't to make light of some truly terrible things. I'm not suggesting they rejoice when their children starve, or their loved ones are murdered, but they are far less inclined to look negatively at the world than we are, despite our relative material prosperity and security.

We don't have to wait until the Kingdom of God comes in its fullness to celebrate the signs we see of it now. We don't have to wait until all is well to celebrate what we already see of love and forgiveness and care – those signs that the Kingdom is at hand. This isn't always easy. As Nouwen says:

"This is a real discipline. It requires choosing for the light even when there is much darkness to frighten me, choosing for life even when the forces of death are so visible, and choosing for the truth even when I am surrounded with lies. I am tempted to be so impressed by the obvious sadness of the human condition that I no longer claim the joy manifesting itself in many small but very real ways. The reward of choosing joy is joy itself. Living among people with mental disabilities has convinced me of that. There is so much rejection, pain, and woundedness among us, but once you choose to claim the joy hidden in the midst of all suffering, life becomes a celebration. Joy never denies the sadness, but transforms it to a fertile soil for more joy."[3]

Faith is a choosing of life despite suffering - refusing to listen to the voices that focus only on the darkness. Nouwen writes from his perspective of living among those with severe disabilities in L'Arche communities.

There, among those the world looks on with fear or pity, he found so much joy. To be told 'How dare you believe in a loving God!' because of the suffering of the world, sounds pretty hollow in that sort of context. Actually, I think there is a darkness behind the atheist refusal to see good despite the suffering. It rests on a philosophical position that would deny that the lives of the seriously disabled are 'worth it'. Atheists would not say, or even think that, I am sure, but that is the logic of the position that denies there can be belief in goodness because of suffering. They are unintentionally arguing that it would be better if the seriously disabled had not been born. Actually, they are arguing that it would be better if none of us (even themselves) had been born. If that's really what they think, OK. But let's be clear about it. I beg to differ.

As I said, we could end up feeling very negative after reading (or writing) such a book as this. We could close the last page and find ourselves grudgingly still believing. Or we could fall by David Hume's question. The existence of a good God may be compatible with such a world, but Is it *likely* given the evidence? That's why I'd like to go further and say that a faith position is more than just compatible with the world as we experience it, but actually it makes far *better* sense than the atheist position.

It has often been pointed out that there is a flip side to the philosophical 'Problem of Evil'. There is an equal and opposite 'Problem of Good'.

Thomas Merton asked;

"… consider how in spite of centuries of sin and greed and lust and cruelty and hatred and avarice and oppression and injustice, spawned and bred by the free wills of men, the human race can still recover, each time, and can still produce men and women who overcome evil with good, hatred with love, greed with charity, lust and cruelty with sanctity. How could all this be possible without the merciful love of God, pouring out his grace upon us?"[4]

If the world is really just a random accident why is there so much good? Why do we experience things that give us no evolutionary benefit – like the stars or mountains or ice crystals – as beautiful? The 'Problem of Beauty' could be a whole other book! Why is there so much love and selflessness, which so often seem to cut against biological imperatives? We care for the seriously disabled in defiance of the survival of the fittest. It's true many societies don't, and arguably haven't been able to afford to, but what is it in us that revolts against this? If there is no God of love it ought to be just common sense.

I would contend that saying the universe is ultimately created by a God of love is not just *compatible* with the world as it is, but actually the best possible explanation, not so much for the world as it is, but for the way we *experience* the world. It is a better 'fit' than the universe as a random accident – because we *care*. We would have no way of saying evil is absolutely 'wrong' if this world was just a chaos. It may not be very nice. We may not like it. We could still respond with compassion, but we *couldn't* say what we feel – that things *shouldn't* be this way. We couldn't rationally have Fry's anger at bone cancer and insects that lay eggs in children's eyes. But we *do*. Fry is absolutely right to have that anger. But the best explanation for that is not just that we're being emotional and irrational, but that we're deeply in tune with something at the heart of the universe that 'groans', as St Paul would put it, for things to be different. That something is love, and God is love.

We don't want to just say that the Holocaust was not very nice. We don't want to just say that the abandoning of the disabled is an unfortunate necessity. We want to say these, and many other things, are *wrong*. They *should not* be. We absolutely condemn evil. This is because it is not compatible with love; and the universe is as it is, with all of its horrors and terrors, because of love. These things are perfectly compatible with an atheist position - just what you would expect in fact. But while that may objectively 'fit' (be compatible) with the facts, it is not how we *experience* the world. We *long* for something better and believe that is more than just wishful thinking. We absolutely condemn evil as *objectively* wrong. This is just what an atheist position cannot do. It can make a good case for what we call 'wrong' or 'evil' as subjective, relative human concepts, but it cannot say what we want to say – that they *should not* be. It is quite possible that we simply want to say this for emotional reasons and it has nothing to do with objective facts; but it somehow doesn't feel right to me to say those who want to absolutely condemn genocide or child murder are just being emotional! A faith position, in this way, fits better with how we experience the world, how we feel about it, and what we want to say about it.

Also, as I have contended already, to abandon faith because of suffering would be to abandon one of the main comforts in suffering and one of the main historical motivators to *combat* suffering. Faith makes a difference. It gives (or ought to give) a motivation to struggle against suffering (rather than just accept that's how things are). Though compassion is an important concept in many religions, it is particularly important in the Christian tradition. T.E. Lawrence in 'The Pillars of Wisdom', told a story of helping a man in trouble in the desert. His companions were going to leave him behind. What's the point, they felt, in risking your own survival by helping another? They simply said, 'It is written' that he will die. The Christian tradition in which Lawrence was raised (whether he personally shared the faith or not) will not allow that. Lawrence helped the man and succeeded in bringing him to safety, then said, "It isn't written until you write it!" While the world as it is may have been allowed by God to exist in the form it does, that is not an argument for accepting it as it is. Rather the Christian vision of the Kingdom of God is all about bringing creation to a better fruition. Creation is as it is because of love, for love could not exist otherwise, but the same love moves creation towards a vision where 'Death will be no more. Mourning and crying and pain will be no more.' (Rev.21:4)

The atheist retort to this has been that religion is the 'opium of the people' (after Karl Marx), and because of its alleged focus on the next life it makes people put up with injustice and suffering instead of fighting against them. I'm sure there is more than a grain of truth in this accusation, at least historically speaking, but the reverse can also be true, and *has* also been true. It is incumbent on people of faith to make sure it is true. The same 'opium of the people' accusation, however, could also be levelled at atheism. Because it believes evil and suffering are simply the natural out-workings of a random universe, there is no sense that things *should not* be otherwise and therefore no motivation (rationally speaking) to fight against them. I recognize that this is an unjust accusation, but the point is that it is no more unjust than levelling it at religion.

Another commonly levelled accusation, and often unthinkingly accepted as true by believers, is that religion is not just negatively irrational, but it positively does bad things. Particularly, it causes wars. Different faith

71

groups have often been at one another's throats. To quote Stephen Fry again, speaking on QI about some historical conflict;

"...Catholic versus Protestant, essentially. It's that kind of fight. ... And it goes on to this day. Will we never learn? Who knows? Religion. Shit it!"[5]

This is a bit of an aside from our main purpose in this book, but as it is another way faith is commonly brow-beaten, and is certainly related, it may be an aside worth exploring.

There do seem to be more than the usual number of terrible wars going on at the moment, and some of them appear, at least on the surface, to be religiously fuelled. It seems to be one of the standard accusations against faith today, that religion causes wars, and most of us, people of faith, tend to agree and find ourselves apologizing. Where it has genuinely been the case, that is appropriate, but I have come to believe that the accusation is mostly the product of lazy thinking that we could very well challenge.

Yes, historically, religious people have often been involved in wars, but historically, almost *all* people have been religious in some shape or form. Arguing that religion causes war is a bit like arguing that eating food causes war, because all the combatants use eating to sustain them in their fight! And, of course, conflict over food or other resources is often a cause of war and all sorts of unpleasantness. And you could widen that thought to take in many of the other evils perpetrated in the name of religion. People who eat do all sorts of terrible things, therefore eating must be a bad thing and needs to be abandoned! Ridiculous of course, but it's the logical equivalent of some of the attacks on religion.

If you could show that where religion is discarded there are fewer wars, and fewer acts of cruelty, *then* a case could be made. But look at the evidence. The last century was the first century we could really say that religion has started to be less universal, and it was the bloodiest century in human history. Our own century is not shaping up too well either.

The most costly wars, in terms of human life, in the 20th Century were World War One, World War Two, the Russian Revolutionary Wars and the Chinese Revolutionary Wars, and not one of these had any significant religious element to it – unless you count atheism as a religion! The atheists who accuse religion of being damaging don't have much to shout about historically. Look at the societies that have seriously tried to manage without religion and what do we find? The Reign of Terror in Revolutionary France, Stalin's Russia, Mao's China, Pol Pot's Cambodia... Not sounding too great so far! And, though it perhaps wasn't so explicitly atheist, Nazism was significantly inspired by the atheist 'God is Dead' philosophy of Nietzsche. In short, we might retort in kind, 'Atheism. Shit it!'

Actually, I wouldn't say that out loud as I think it is unkind... but I will leave it in print! Why? Because of all those believers who have heard those words levelled at them and almost felt guilty about their faith because of them. It is not fair to many good and honest atheists, but it is no *more* unfair than the accusations they level at religion. Faith is not just compatible with the world as it is. It is better than that. Without being proud of where faith has been misused and misrepresented, we can, I believe, be confident that faith is a rational and good response to the realities of this world, and we have the resources within faith and reason to stand up to our detractors.

If religion causes wars, it seems atheism causes worse wars. There *have* been wars that were significantly fuelled by religion, like the Crusades (though arguably they were really a land grab, religiously justified), or the 30 years war in the 17th Century (though the causes of that were very complex). And some of the current conflicts seem to have a religious element to them – Jewish Zionism versus fundamentalist Islam in Israel – but again it seems to be more about land than religion. And then there's the so-called Islamic State in Iraq, Syria and Libya but that is condemned by religious people of all colours. Just because there have been extreme atheists who killed millions in the name of their ideology doesn't mean we can tar all atheists with the same brush. In the same way the existence of the 'Islamic State' extremism is not in itself an argument against religion.

Religion is certainly a powerful motivator, and it gives courage to those fighting injustice (real or perceived), and, in its fundamentalist forms, it can lead to claiming God is on your side and hating your enemies. Foul deeds *can* certainly be done in the name of God, but that is really taking the name of the Lord in vain. Religion also gives strength to those working for peace. What strength does atheism give?

Let's let our faith challenge us to work for peace, and not be put off it by the accusations of those who haven't thought their history through.

I'd like to turn in to the final straight of this book with a reflection on joy. That might seem odd in a book about the most terrible things life can throw at us, but I think it is central if this book is to be a 'Christian' response, which is what I have aimed at. Faith is not just compatible with the world as it is, so we can sigh and carry on. It's better than that. It's not all bad! Look around you. Open your eyes to how much good there is.

Parts of the Bible, particularly the Psalms and passages from Paul's letters, seem to fizz with joy and rejoicing. But as human beings (particularly English ones!) we often seem content in our conversation to outdo one another with how hard we find life. We'd rather speak about how horribly busy we are, or how many bad things we have to deal with. We are 'glass half-empty' people. Even as Christians we don't show much evident joy. I know I often don't.

Reflect for a moment on the story of Paul and Silas in prison in Philippi in Acts 16:25-34. Having been flogged and imprisoned for helping someone, they sang in their stocks and chains. I don't think they were feeling particularly cheerful or smiling with cheesy grins at that moment – joy is something much deeper than an emotional feeling of happiness. But in a dark situation in a dark world they found it in themselves to sing, and that made them free. Their prison broke open. For Paul, even when he felt his life was being 'poured out' as he wrote from another prison, he still talked about having learned to be content in all circumstances and said, 'Rejoice in the Lord always. I will say it again: Rejoice!' (Phil.2:17; 4:4,12) But he wasn't speaking about a quick anti-depressive emotional injection, temporarily ignoring the realities of the world or our situation. He wasn't recommending being a stupid grinning Pollyanna; he was talking about a profound spiritual *discipline*. Anyone who has seriously tried Christianity will be used to thinking of the other so-called 'fruits of the Spirit' as disciplines – love, peace, gentleness, self-control – they require effort. But we tend to assume that joy must just happen – either you have it or you don't. We think it is dependent on external circumstances.

No. Joy requires hard work, and courage. It must not be about ignoring the realities of the world around us, or making light of terrible things, but about experiencing them so deeply that, in the midst of them, we can trace the face and the form of the crucified one. Joy is not about counting our blessings and over-looking the rest – it is about meeting God in the midst of adverse circumstances. That doesn't mean we can be joyful *about* terrible tragedies, or content with the state of the world; but even if everything else is taken away from us, we can still find God, and that is enough.

This is a powerful weapon against what Paul called 'the principalities and powers' of this age. It is a way of standing up to the consumer society which is parasitical on the conditions of dissatisfaction that it creates. To be joyful in this way is to know that there is nothing we can buy that can make us more content. Joy, in this way, can even be politically radical – no longer being tempted by the promises of politicians to make us more financially comfortable, or by threats to take away our external liberties. Joy is deeply counter-cultural and attractive. It liberates us from addiction to a life of predictable comfort, if we can be joyful without that.

Joy is seen most clearly against the background of adverse circumstances, when we think that, by all rights, people in those situations ought not to be joyful - when people can be joyful from a position of weakness rather than strength. This is what strikes travellers from our joyless culture so powerfully when they travel in the 'Developing' world. Is it our blindness to this sort of joy that makes the existence of suffering so difficult for us to reconcile with goodness and love?

The danger with talking about joy in the face of suffering in this way is that we must not be dishonest. Joy is not pretending. It is not gritting our teeth and forcing ourselves to thank God for the many evils in this world, against our better judgement. The discipline is about consciously *searching* for elements of joy in each and every situation. Sometimes we may not, in all honesty, be able to find them. I'm not suggesting that we search for the joy in the death of a child for example; though some can even manage that – being able to find a sense of contentment, perhaps, in the fact their suffering is over, or being able to still find joy in the inappropriate antics of their other children. I am personally familiar with wanting to laugh with joy and cry with grief and horror at the same time. The two are not mutually exclusive, even though they feel incongruous. Though there are things in which we cannot rejoice, that doesn't mean all the rest of the world is dark. This is an area to tread very carefully in. It can run into the same danger as seeking the sort of answers that might let us be content with the existence of suffering and evil. It is not OK. God does not think it is OK. But *some* things being not OK does not mean *everything* is not OK.

How far can this joy go? I don't pretend to know. Was Jesus joyful on the cross? If joy is a gift and discipline of the Spirit? I think perhaps he was – his deep contentment in his Father could exist even in the midst of the cry of dereliction...? Perhaps. I can't plumb those depths. But if he *wasn't* joyful there I am comforted that he has shared our loss of joy. If he *was* joyful there I am comforted that his joy could overcome the darkest depths. From St Paul's experience, his rejoicing in the Lord was not incompatible with being poured out (Phil.2:17). His joy was the context in which whatever was to his profit he considered loss compared to the surpassing greatness of knowing Christ as his Lord. (Phil.3:7) Joy is the context in which the peace of God which passes all understanding guards our hearts and minds in Christ Jesus. Joy is the context in which we think of whatever is good, true and lovely – for despite the horrors of existence there *are* such things. (Phil.4:7-8)

It is my hope that this book will help you understand that your faith need not be threatened by the existence of suffering. Rather faith is, or can be, a response to suffering. We don't have to just hold uncomfortably to belief – our faith like a square peg in the round hole of this world. Rather we can live with and reflect on this faith, which was *born* out of deep reflection on suffering – born out of deep engagement with reality as it is. Real faith is about wrestling. Suffering doesn't threaten real faith. It threatens pagan-like beliefs which think of faith as a deal with God or an insurance against trouble. It didn't work that way for Jesus and it won't work that way for anyone else. I'm not suggesting that I have achieved 'real faith' in this sense, or that it is something every believer can easily possess, but it is something I struggle to attain to. Or perhaps, more properly, it is something I pray for and wait for as a gift that only God can give. Suffering doesn't threaten 'real faith' - it deepens it. It can even give birth to it.

It may seem paradoxical, but for many people the experience of suffering actually *creates* faith. I recall a parishioner I knew, who came to faith because of the Boxing Day tsunami of 2004. I don't recall his exact reasons – I don't think he'd worked them out fully himself – but it was something to do with a new perspective it gave him on life, based on the compassion he felt, which would have made no sense if the universe were just a meaningless accident. The broadcaster Rabbi Hugo Gryn (1930-1996) had his first experience of God in a Nazi concentration camp, as a 17 year-old, hiding in a corner of the camp he wept for himself and the Jewish race and the whole world and felt, for the first time, the reality and 'otherness' of God. As he was to say later, "Evil is real. So is Good."[6] Fellow believers of other faiths find that they meet God in and through suffering too, though I personally don't understand how they hold to it if God doesn't suffer, but their experience is real enough. Faith is not about making life easier (intellectually or physically) – it's about making it more real.

Whenever I have heard powerful arguments against faith that use evil and suffering as the basis for denying a God of love, while I can recognise and feel their power, I have always had a strange feeling that they fundamentally miss the point. I can nod along in agreement with Stephen Fry in his passionate objections, and then carry on praying. I don't think this is because I am being a 'fideist' – that is someone who holds a philosophical position, consciously or otherwise, that believes faith is a different realm from that of reason, so rational objections have no bearing on faith. I had the same experience when our daughter was stillborn. Though I grieved deeply, and what had happened was deeply relevant to my faith, it didn't destroy my faith but somehow slid off it – leaving its mark, but leaving faith intact. For me faith has always been about belief in a God who suffered for the world he loves. Suffering and sorrow was always potentially part of the 'deal' because faith is a response to the world as it is. And while rationally wrestling things through is part of loving God with all your mind, faith doesn't depend on getting it all 'straight' in your head. You never will, because we don't live in a 'straight' world in that sense. Arguments about free will and love only being possible in this sort of world have merit, but I have never found them wholly satisfying. But faith doesn't depend on them, it depends, for the Christian, on Jesus.

Not that we sit back and rest comfortable with the existence of suffering, but rather we try to pick up the tools to live with it, wrestle with it, fight against it. But we do that always remembering that, though there is suffering, there is also love.

And perhaps there is suffering *because* of love.

Epilogue

In the days immediately after losing our Hannah we were very raw. There were tears. But the thing that kept me going was our three year-old son. He was confused that the sister we had told him was coming, and we had long been preparing him for, now wasn't coming; but, as three year-olds will, he largely carried on regardless, with his needs for fun and food and care, which we had to meet. But he did ask questions. 'Why?' ... of course. Where was she now? Didn't know how to answer that... still don't... at least not without a whole other book that ends without satisfying answers. We said, 'She's with Jesus.' That led to its own comic moments, like when he asked the undertaker, when we went to see her in the chapel of rest, 'Are you Jesus?!' Try explaining suffering to a three year-old and you'll understand that there aren't really intellectual answers, because this isn't an intellectual problem.

But there was one question he asked that has been, for me, an answer. One night, a day or two after the event, when putting him to bed, after some tears from us, and being told, again, she was with Jesus, he asked one final question...

'Is Jesus crying?' ... 'Yes.' I choked out. Yes...

....

"When pain is to be borne, a little courage helps much more than knowledge, a little human sympathy more than much courage and the least tincture of the love of God more than all." [1]

C.S. Lewis

Notes

Prologue

1. Eduard Schweizer, 'Jesus Christ the man from Nazareth and the exalted Lord: the 1984 Sizemore...' 1989 p.59

Introduction

1. Posted on The Huffington Post website 30.1.15

Chapter One

1. C.S. Lewis, Surprised by Joy, Collins (Fontana Books), 1959, p.94-95

2. A survey of different nations' attitudes to matters of faith presented on ITV some years back asked, among many other things, whether the existence of suffering was a barrier to belief. This question scored very highly in the Western world but scored very low in poorer nations.

3. C.S. Lewis, 'A Grief Observed', (Faber & Faber, 1961), p.23

4. David Hume, 'Dialogues Concerning Natural Religion' (Part XI), Penguin Classic, (1990) p.115. My emphasis.

5. Levellers, 'Is This Art?' from the album 'Levellers', released 1993

Chapter Two

1. Ludwig Wittgenstein, Culture and Value, ed. G.H. Von Wright with Heikki Nyman, trans. P. Winch (Oxford: Basil Blackwell, 1980), 86e-87e

2. Fyodor Dostoyevsky, 'The Brothers Karamazov' (Trans, David Magarshack), Penguin Classics, 1958, p.287

3. Romans 8:18 I don't believe Paul is dealing with an abstract philosophical question of whether suffering can be weighed against reward in heaven. He's speaking about our experience of that glory revealed *in us,* as we find a bigger perspective than our sufferings now, not in some future heaven.

4. In an interview in 'Inspire' magazine (Issue 86, March 2014, published by CPO)

Chapter Four

1. Richard Holloway, 'Dancing on the Edge' (Fount, 1997), p.167

2. Rodney Holder describes this in an Advent reflection in 'Longing, Waiting, Believing' (BRF, 2014)

Chapter Five

1. See Tom Wright, 'Reflecting the Glory' (Bible Reading Fellowship, 1997) for a Lenten Bible study on this.

2. John Hick wrote much about this idea, giving a modern take on the Second Century theodicy of Irenaeus.

3. See the so-called 'Servant Songs': Isa.42:1-4; 49:1-6; 50:4-9; 52:13-53:12 & possibly 63:1-3

Chapter Six

1. Geoffrey Studdert-Kennedy, 'The Unutterable Beauty' (Hodder & Stoughton, 1968) p.12 – originally published in 1927

2. Jürgen Moltmann, 'The Crucified God' (SCM Press Ltd, 1974), p.274

3. C.S. Lewis, the last verse of the poem, 'Love's as warm as tears' in Malcolm Guite, 'Word in the Wilderness' (Canterbury Press, 2014), p.148

Chapter Seven

1. Peter Kreeft, 'Making Sense out of Suffering' (London: Hodder & Stoughton, 1986) p.146

2. Charles Dickens, 'A Christmas Carol' published in 1843, near the beginning of Stave II (In my copy, Puffin, 1984, p.33)

3. Rowan Williams,

https://www.theguardian.com/uk/2005/jan/03/tsunami2004.world

Chapter Eight

1. Henri J.M. Nouwen, 'The Return of the Prodigal Son' (Darton, Longman & Todd, 1992) p.114 after Luke 15:7,10

2. *ibid* p.115

3. *ibid* p.115-116

4. Thomas Merton in 'The Seven Storey Mountain', quoted in 'Advent and Christmas with Thomas Merton (Redemptorist, Liguori, Missouri, 2002) p.5

5. http://www.goodreads.com/quotes/tag/stephen-fry

6. http://www.hugogryn.com/about-hugo-gryn/ The story of Gryn's experience is related by his friend Adrian Plass in his book of reflections, 'When You Walk' (Bible Reading Fellowship, 1997), p.73

Epilogue

1. C.S. Lewis, 'The Problem of Pain' (Glasgow: Collins, Fount, 1940) p.9

Printed in Germany
by Amazon Distribution
GmbH, Leipzig